John Jay Janney's
VIRGINIA

John Jay Janney's
VIRGINIA

An American Farm Lad's Life
in the Early 19th Century

Asa Moore Janney
Werner L. Janney, Editors

EPM Publications, Inc.

McLean Virginia

Library of Congress Cataloging in Publication Data
Janney, John Jay, 1812-1907.
    John Jay Janney's Virginia.

    Bibliography: p.
    1. Janney, John Jay, 1812-1907. 2. Loudoun
Co., Va.—Biography. 3. Friends, Society of—
Virginia—Loudoun Co.—Biography. 4. Lincoln,
Abraham, Pres. U.S., 1809-1865. 5. Country
life—Virginia—Loudoun Co. I. Janney, Asa
Moore. II. Janney, Werner L. III. Title.
IV. Title: Virginia.
F232.L8J32 1978   975.5'28'03   78-23319
ISBN: 0-914440-25-X

EPM Publications, Inc., 1003 Turkey Run Road,
McLean, Virginia 22101
Printed in the United States of America

Design and Illustrations by Martha Vaughan and Laurel Vaughan

Cover by Laurel Vaughan

THE JANNEY FAMILY TREE

TABLE OF CONTENTS

OFF TO OHIO

Inheritance, schooling in Alexandria, trip to Ohio with a prairie schooner, teaching school, settling in Warren County, keeping store, surveying, law, clerking in House, clerking for the Secretary of State, clerking for Board of Control of State Bank of Ohio, secretary-treasurer of Columbus-Hocking Valley Railroad, civic offices and services, secretary-treasurer of Republic State Committee, public library, life draws to a close

ABOUT JOHN JAY JANNEY

It was John Jay Janney's education that allows us the present glimpse of the life lived by those people of early 19th century Virginia who were not of the aristocracy and could not qualify for the Establishment. Except in areas where religious denominations such as the Quakers who taught John had private schools, the words educated and rich were synonymous. We know therefore how those lived who owned and administered the great plantations of Tidewater Virginia. Where slave labor brought wealth and culture to a small class, there were leisure and skills sufficient to the writing of letters, journals and diaries.

The jottings of other Americans have not fared so well: Any scribbled bits left behind by "poor whites" were hardly thought worth the reading, let alone the saving. What of the "middle class"? That term would not have been heard at that time. Then what of the "sturdy yeomen" who ran farms of a hundred acres or so, just large enough for the family and a few hired hands to work? What do we know of the women who had but lately left a log cabin for the comfort of a small, snug fieldstone house?

John's recollections of country life 150 years ago help fill the gap. He was scantily clothed and he worked by his uncle's side as hard as his frail body would allow, but he did get an education. And fortunately for us, when in later days he was spurred to put down on paper the details of life in a backwoods community, his words were saved intact. Though the three versions of his memoirs have been merged here, his syntax and spellings have been left as he wrote them. It is the first time that any of the three have been presented to the general public.

In 1907, in his final year of life, old John Janney was laid up in his room in Columbus, Ohio, with a game leg, kidney trouble, and rheumatism; but he got a brand new blankbook and wrote down his boyhood memories. He had read several books by an indefatigable investigator of colonial life,

Mrs. Alice Morse Earle. She had assembled the stuff of colonial existence: hair styles, dress, cooking methods, punishments, anything at all about the day-to-day life of children and adults in pre-Revolutionary America. John liked her books and observed that the young people of his own last days knew little more about how he had lived in his youth than he had known about the colonists. He set out to rectify matters.

He had already written down his recollections for his grandchildren and their half-sisters, but the book had been lost and so he gamely started recopying his original draft. As he thought of his youth, he remembered what it had been to be a boy on a small Virginia farm, where everybody had a job to do and no machinery to do it except what the blacksmith could contrive. He remembered what it had been like not even to have a stove, so that the cooking and heating all came from the kitchen fireplace. He remembered what it had been like when the passenger pigeons flew over in flocks a mile wide, and how folks had acted when Nat Turner raised his slave insurrection 200 miles to the south. He remembered what it had been like to plant and tread out grain with horse power, to spin and weave with woman and girl power, and to pound hominy with man and boy power. He remembered the flour you got by taking your own farm-grown wheat down to the mill, and how your coat came from sheep you had known and become fond of.

He remembered all the games the young people had played—the kissing games, the sports with balls, the elder-squirts and kites. Finally he remembered what it had been like to grow up as one of the Quakers, or peculiar people. They lived simply and went, still simply, in the backs of wagons to their graves.

Remembering all these things, he wrote about them in his lonely room, where all he now saw of life was what passed by beneath his window. Before he died, he closed his book, satisfied he had done as well as he could in preserving the details of an ordinary farmer's life in the 1820's.

John Janney was pretty old when he died in 1907. To look at it one way, he was born the year that the War of 1812 opened, and when he died, the First World War was staring from around the corner. Or, put it that he was born three years before the Battle of Waterloo, while James Madison was working at being the fifth President of the United States, and died while Teddy Roosevelt was being vital as the 26th. Or, if we want, when he was born there were two ways of getting places on land: you walked or you got a horse. By the time he died, railroads were rushing people all around the continent, headlines were already reporting deaths from speeding autos, and the Wright brothers were starting the age of planes.

In 1812, John's part of northern Virginia was provincial or even backwoodsy. Cut off on the west by the Blue Ridge, cut off from commerce to the south by the three-day journey needed for hauling goods over atrocious roads from the navigable waters of the Potomac, cut off on the north and east by the same river, whose stream could be crossed only on inadequate ferries—isolated in every direction, the people of Loudoun County were living and would be living for years in fundamentally the same kind of rural culture that they and their parents had known during the Revolution. (Indeed, for a few more years George III was still to sit on the throne of England.) Down to the antiquated knee britches worn by older men, Loudouners in John's boyhood were living in a traditional agrarian society, one that was badly affected by the Napoleonic depression then reigning. Loudoun's young men—those with spirit—were fleeing from that depression to the beckoning west, *i.e.* Ohio. In 1831 John Janney too would head west, just before the advent of a toll turnpike and the Chesapeake and Ohio Canal would at last make the outside world available to Loudouners.

John was the third generation of his family born in Loudoun County. Sixty-seven years before his birth, Jacob and Hannah Janney had come down from Pennsylvania in a covered wagon and had hewed a farm out of the wilderness. The Janneys were among the first to enter the Goose Creek neighborhood, and Hannah made certain that the family name would spread over much of the county by giving Jacob twelve children. She was a redoubtable minister too, and is credited with starting the Goose Creek Quaker Meeting on a log in the unbroken forest. The Meeting is still in business more than 225 years later, and growing in numbers.

John was born into a Quaker community still so close to primeval wilderness that folks could see patches of it all around, but established enough so that farming set the pattern of the daily round. Everything was done by hand, of course, or by hand and by horse, and on workdays everybody fell exhausted into an early bed. On Sunday or, as they would have put it, on First Day, Friends spent several hours in a Meeting for Worship. The silence was broken only by those who were urged to speak by a Power beyond their powers but not beyond their reach, a Power that they felt quite comfortable with. On Thursday, called Fifth Day, there was another Meeting for Worship in the afternoon. Attendance at these Meetings was so regular that even dogs complied. On one Fifth Day when a member hitched up his horse to go to Meeting and went back into the house and died instead, his dog waited only a while before trotting off to town without him and spent the Meeting hour in its accustomed spot under the bench.

Friends believed in direct inspiration from God, and uniting the spiritual with the practical, they also believed in basic education. Save for Sundays and a few weeks during harvest, Friends' children were sent to school every day of the year, Christmas not excepted. No Latin or foreign languages, no enriched curriculum were taught. John and his classmates studied such subjects as English and mathematics, and got their toes wet in algebra. They studied history and geography too—and this at a time when many non-Friends were growing up around them able neither to read nor to write. Public education, as noted above, was hardly a popular cause among the aristocrats of Virginia who could hire their own tutors and were happier when members of the lower classes were kept in their places. In the midst of slavery, the Quakers even allowed black children to attend their schools.

Whatever the cause, Friends were then a clannish sect and kept to themselves. Members were disowned for "marrying out of Meeting," as the editors' grandfather could testify after he married a Methodist. Rather as the early Mormons are pictured, Friends would associate with others but hardly consort with them. Friends prided themselves on being a peculiar people unto the Lord, who did not seek converts and were content to draw in upon themselves. In later years John, who had gone west at the first opportunity, would look back with a gentle wonder on the Quakers of Goose Creek.

The Goose Creek Quakers' first meeting house was of logs, supplanted in 1765 by one of stone; in 1817 the stone house was succeeded by the present ample structure of brick. This last one cost $3,500 (collected in cash before work was begun) plus an additional $500 given to the contractor when he had finished, because the meeting thought he had not allowed himself enough profit.

The meeting house's succession of logs, stone, and brick recapitulated the story of many a private dwelling nearby. Some of these are still standing today, with all three buildings—of logs, stone, and brick—joined end to end and going from smallest to largest like an expanded telescope.

The house where John was born in 1812 was different. It had been erected in 1785 or thereabouts by his grandfather Blackstone Janney, son of Jacob the settler. Blackstone daringly built it all of brick to begin with and was roundly criticized for his extravagance. When Blackstone's son Eli later needed an addition, he discreetly made it of ordinary fieldstone, as we can see today.

Deed books show that when John was born to Thomas Jefferson Janney and his young wife Mary Taylor Janney, Blackstone still owned the house and farm, though he and his wife had left the place for town life in Goose Creek, near the Quaker meeting house. A month after John's birth his father died, leaving his bride a widow only two weeks after their first anniversary. John's mother wasted no time in returning with her baby to her own parents, Mahlon K. and Mary Taylor.

Three years later John's Uncle Eli Janney bought John's birthplace from his and Thomas Jefferson's father. Eli had been thrown out of meeting for marrying a girl who was not a Quaker, or, as the Goose Creek Meeting of Friends charitably phrased it, for "fornication with her that is now his wife." Even when she died and Eli took a second wife, this time a proper Quaker, he still did not return to the Friendly fold. When he took John, later on, to live with him in the house of the boy's birth, John's mother could stand the contamination for only two years. She then haled her son back to her mother's on the plea that he might learn bad language if he stayed. This sounds like a trumped-up excuse; John obviously could be allowed only so much association with a backslider.

The Taylor farm was a good one, and it still is, under its present owner. Within the lifetime of John's elders, a local revolution in agriculture had occurred that was to affect first the county, then the entire nation. As John himself tells us, when his grandparents, the Taylors, got their farm, it was already considered worn-out, but by careful management they restored it to productivity. Most of their neighbors would also have been exercising the same careful management, for they too would have been practicing the new Loudoun System of farming. Two Loudouners, John Binns and Israel Janney, John's great-uncle, had introduced an upheaval beyond our imaginings when they rehabilitated their worn-out land with a regimen that included applying gypsum and lime, planting clover, plowing deep, and rotating their crops. Binns had spread the new gospel by publishing a little booklet nine years before John was born. The Loudoun System worked so phenomenally well that it spread rapidly across the county, bringing back into full production many a worked-out farm like the Taylor's. President Jefferson himself promoted the System abroad, and it eventually became the standard American method of farming and lost the name of "Loudoun." John might have been worked to a frazzle on his grandparents' farm, but it was a good farm, and practically all the Friends and other landowners of the region were prosperous farmers for their day.

As we go through the pages of John's memoirs, we gradually become aware of an unusual vagueness on his part about the names of his immediate family. He does name his Uncle Eli, the backslider. He names a procession of local drunks, two hired men (one an idiot, the other afraid of ghosts), a dying doctor, a cousin he played with, the dogs, his horse. . . . But we learn the names of his father and his father's father almost by accident when John is nearly through his book and ready to leave home. We look in vain for the names of the maternal grandparents who raised him and in whose home he lived for most of 21 years. And, crowning touch, not once does John write the name of his mother!

It is only from other sources that we learn the names of his supposed nearest and dearest. Quaker records of the time tell us that John's mother, Mary Taylor Janney, married a second time when the boy was but seven years old — and we suddenly understand. John's mother married a widower and went off to take care of his children, leaving her own young son with her parents. Mary gave Seth Smith two more children—and John never whispers about either his two half-sisters or their father. It takes no Freud to spot a youngster who felt himself deserted by a father who left him when he was but a month old, deserted by his mother when he was seven, left with grandparents who acquiesced in the desertion, and not allowed even to stay with the uncle who wished to keep him and educate him.

John's failure to mention the names of the family that he himself started seems to rest on a different footing. In 1835, when he was 23, he married his stepsister, Rebecca Smith. John does not mention her by name, nor do we learn from him of his five children, nor of his nine grandchildren—save for the two youngest whose deaths he records in a note. In 1907, when John was writing his last lines in Ohio, his wife and all his children were dead and only two of his grandchildren were still living, one in Pennsylvania, one out West. According to family tradition there was no one left in Columbus to see to the old man except a son-in-law and a step-granddaughter. John may not have been able to blot out painful memories, but he was adequate to the job of keeping them from cluttering his pages.

Though the greatest part of his account covers only the first 19 years of John's life, the final few pages tell us a bit of what happened in his later years. From Loudoun, John left for Ohio in 1831, walking beside a prairie schooner. When he got there, he worked at teaching, surveying, and just about anything that needed the education so many people didn't have. Later, however, he jumped into the promising waters of public service and acquitted himself ably, though he never set the world on fire. After a little clerking for the State House of Representatives, he moved on to several years in the office of the Ohio Secretary of State and Commissioner of Common Schools, then to 15 more as Secretary of the Board of Control of the State Bank of Ohio, and then to another 15 as Secretary of the Columbus and Hocking Valley Railroad. Along the way he served his adopted city of Columbus in many ways, including a couple of years on the City Council.

A 164-page journal at the University of California, Berkeley, and 21 boxes of his family papers held by the Ohio Historical Society give added glimpses of his life in Columbus: assistant postmaster, chairman of first the Whig and then the Republican city and county committees, member of the Board of Education, a director of the Ohio Penitentiary, treasurer of the Prisoners Aid Society, an inveterate foe of slavery, liquor, tobacco and war, and a champion of free public schools and women's suffrage.

He was proud of fathering the city's free library—a claim that not everybody allowed him, as he admits with some asperity.

After the dedication of the Carnegie Library on April 4, 1907, one city newspaper reported fulsomely: "Bowed beneath the weight of almost a century of years, J. J. Janney, 'the father of the Columbus Public Library,' had the pleasure of seeing at last the purpose of his life acomplished and the satisfaction of addressing the audience which gathered at the dedication exercises of the Columbus Public Library Thursday after- noon. . . . The most impressive part of the exercises came when Mr. Janney was assisted to the platform by two friends and addressed the audience. Old and infirm, with hair as white as the driven snow, but still in possession of all his faculties, Mr. Janney spoke, in a voice weak and quavering, of the trials and tribulations which have marked the lives of the early advocates of the public library." Another paper, however — perhaps of a different political persuasion? — had only the following spare paragraph at the very end of its lengthy account, where the make-up man would have dropped it if the story hadn't fit the page: "J. J. Janney who probably is the oldest man now living who has been identified with the library work, spoke at some length. Mr. Janney is 95, but still spoke with considerable distinctness, and shows a surprising memory."

Last of all in his ledger, John entered his interviews with Abraham Lincoln, whom he had met on several occasions as secretary of the fledgling Ohio Republican Party. Incensed at a Collector of Internal Revenue who was not properly observing the principles of the spoils system, he thought it perfectly natural to go to Washington and get an introduction from the President to the Commissioner of Internal Revenue, so he could get such perfidy stopped. When a son-in-law got into trouble by trying to make a little honest money through his Army connections, John again used his acquaintance with Lincoln to have him restored to his position. John tucked away his recollections of Lincoln as an addendum to his text and they are included at the end of this book.

John Janney died on December 11, 1907, leaving behind him three slightly differing copies of his book. One is now at the Bancroft Library of the University of California at Berkeley. The other two copies were inherited by Mr. Edmund D. Haigler of Hatboro, Pennsylvania, a descendant of John's step-granddaughter. About 1970 Mrs. Haigler wrote James Birchfield, now editor of the *Loudoun Times-Mirror*, asking if there actually was a town called Lincoln (the modern name of Goose Creek), as she couldn't find it on any map. Also, were there any Janneys still around? He assured her that there were both, and put her in touch with the senior editor of the present work, the postmaster and storekeeper at Lincoln. Hence this book. Thank you, Mrs. Haigler.

The two editors, who are brothers and John's second cousins twice removed, grew up in the 1920's in the same neighborhood where John had been raised a century earlier, in the 1820's. As boys we attended the same Quaker Meeting that so bored poor John. Both of us, like John, have remained members of the Society of Friends, and one of us, on most Sunday mornings, still goes through the same doors that opened for John so long ago. The two of us are just about a century younger than John, one being junior to him by 96 years, the other by a hundred years and a half. We hope you will excuse us for putting in a personal note every now and then, to let you know how life in the 1820's compared to life in the same community a century later. We are a little staggered to realize how minimally things had changed. The name Goose Creek had become Lincoln, in a successful bid to get a post office in 1861. A few tractors and a little power machinery had come along, and some autos, of course, but otherwise things went ambling along very much as John had described them. The major differences, such as the greater use of fertilizers and the institution of compulsory education for everyone, are more apparent to us now than they would have been to us as boys.

Help has come to us from several sources; first of all, of course, from Mr. and Mrs. Edmund D. Haigler, who own the original documents. On the scene in Loudoun, we sought help and were cheerfully given it by Mr. John G. Lewis, who with his wife, Elisabeth Lewis, has written a history of John's birthplace, *The Minor Bartlow House, 1744-1970.* Mr. Lewis, a restoration consultant, not only carried out the restoration of John's birthplace but owns and lives in the house. He is also the Regional Representative of the Virginia Historic Landmarks Commission and has given advice on several parts of this work. He has especially thrown light on various aspects of John's early homes and his two families.

Last of all, we wish to acknowledge gratefully the permission extended us by the Bancroft Library of the University of California at Berkeley, and by Miss Estelle Rebec, Head of its Manuscripts Division, to use the passages quoted from the John Jay Janney manuscript now held at the Bancroft Library. These are identified in the bibliographical and textual notes.

Asa Moore Janney

Werner L. Janney

JOHN JANNEY'S PREFATORY NOTE

Mr. S.C. Derby, my son in law, handed me a card on which he had suggested the propriety of my writing a sketch of my early life. He thought it would be interesting to the children, referring to his children,* and my grand-children Dorothy and Walter.** After I had written about one hundred pages, Dorothy, ten years old, died suddenly, which seemed to take the interest out of my biography. I afterwards resumed it, and after I had completed it, Walter was drowned, which took away the purpose of my writing. But upon submitting what I had written to some of my friends, they thought it interesting and the original having been destroyed, I have here rewritten it.

----

*Derby's children by his first marriage: Florence Harlow Derby (Mrs. C.E. Haigler, 1873-1956), and Alice Greenwood Derby (Mrs. O.E. Carr, 1878-1945).

**Derby's children by his marriage to John Janney's daughter Frances: Walter Janney Derby (1884-1903), and Dorothy Frances Derby (1889-1900).

AUTOBIOGRAPHY OF JOHN J. JANNEY

How a Family of Quakers Lived in Virginia
1812-1831

John's birthplace as it looks today. Courtesy of John G. Lewis, owner.

I was born April 25th 1812, and my father died May 25th, the day I was a month old, so that I have no recollection of a father, and never had the care of one. After I was married and living in Columbus, I went to my home one evening and found the family at supper with a stranger at the table, who was introduced to me as Gideon Davis. He made nearly all the plows used in the neighborhood, and he was known by every one. I said I had known his name all my life but had never met him before. His reply was that he had never seen me, but he heard me cry once. "I staid with thy father the night before his death. Thy mother came into the room, and I heard a baby cry in the next room. Thy father asked her if she could not keep that baby from crying. She said she could not, he was not well and she could not keep him quiet." He said he had never seen me, nor never heard me afterwards.

Another incident in relation to my father was curious. When I was about fourteen years old, I was at dinner one day and just opposite me sat an elderly woman who knew my father well. Suddenly she looked across the table at me and said "John, thee reminds me so much of thy father. I never saw any person spread his bread and butter as he did, until I saw thee do it. He used to spread the butter as thin as he could, and thee does it just as he did." I have no doubt I inherited that taste from my father.

I never learned any thing about my father. I never knew him, and as a child I felt no interest in him; and no one ever talked to me about him. His father and mother lived till I was about ten years old and I was frequently at their house, as they lived in sight of the school house which I attended.

I was born about two miles South-east of Goose Creek Meeting House, now Lincoln, Loudoun County, Virginia. My birth was in the first brick house built in that neighborhood. The tradition in the family was that the bricks of which the house was built were brought from England, but I recently saw an essay in which the writer says bricks were never imported. I think the evidence is against him. I spent the winter of 1830 in Alexandria, which was at that time a great market for flour. The Shenandoah valley was the great wheat region of the country and Alexandria was the market for it. I have seen ships there from European cities being loaded with flour; and they frequently came "in ballast" as seamen say, that is, without any cargo. They may have come in ballast from Europe. In order to sail, they must have ballast, which was usually sand and gravel from the seashore. It cost something to load and unload the ballast, and if they could buy bricks so that they could sell them for what they paid, it would be better than to pay for ballast. And the farmers, when they hauled a load of flour to Alexandria, could take home a load of bricks without the hauling costing them anything. The bricks of my father's house were certainly not made of the clay of that neighborhood. That always burned into a bright red brick, while they were of a light chocolate color; and besides, they were filled with small bits of a peculiar sand not found there.

> John's case is weak. Shipowners did not clutter their holds with cheap brick when they could ballast their vessels with cargo such as export china, which brought a good price upon docking. Imported brick would have been available close to the wharves, if anyplace, and yet not one building in either Georgetown or Alexandria can be shown to be constructed of that material. If thriving seaports had no houses of imported brick, what of a backwoods farm at the end of a 45-mile haul along unimproved roads?

After my father's death, my mother went back to her father's home, and there I lived until in my twentieth year, except two years with an uncle.

> Though John never names his mother for us, Quaker records tell us that she was Mary Taylor Janney, wife of Thomas Jefferson Janney and daughter of Mahlon K. Taylor, Sr., and Mary Stokes Taylor. The Taylor farm to which she brought her baby was known as Rural Felicity. In a note to the editors, John G. Lewis reports that a Mutual Assurance policy dated in 1803 shows the family to have been living in a "Stone Two Story House 21 x 28," shingled in wood, with a one story wing (the older cabin) built of wood, 18 x 23. The place is marked "M.K. Taylor's heirs" on Yardley Taylor's *Map of Loudoun County, Virginia, from Actual Surveys,* 1853. The fire that John mentions a few pages later, and the passage of time, have erased all traces of the Taylor buildings except the ruins of the springhouse, whose old stone walls stand crumbling beside Route 7 on the eastern approach to Purcellville. W. Curtis Cole owns the place now, but the town is sweeping in on it.

I remember an incident that occurred when I was less than two years old. I was the first and only child and my mother allowed me to use her breast very late. I remember one day worrying her for my dinner, at a time when she was trying to wean me. Finally, she called me to her, and upon baring her breast, I saw she had covered her nipples with soot from the "backwall" of the fire place.

I went to school at the Quaker school, two miles off, commencing before I was six years old and continuing until I was fifteen, after which I worked on the farm in the summer four years. At one time my uncle Eli offered to take me to his house and educate me, and I was with him two years, when my mother insisted on my leaving there, fearing I might learn to swear, of which there was no danger because I had no inclination that way. I went back to my grandmother's, which brought me in close contact with a vulgar, lascivious girl whose influence on me has been a curse to me all my life.

Lafayette visited the United States in 1824 when I was twelve years old. We had notice that he would visit Leesburg, Virginia on a certain day, and my uncle with whom I was living took me there to see him. He staid the night before with ex-president James Monroe at his residence, Oak Hill, near Aldie, and we went to a point on the road at which a cannon was placed to fire a salute. Lafayette and Monroe came in an open carriage and I saw both at close range but when we reached the court house where the reception took place, the house and grounds were so packed that we could neither see nor hear any part of the ceremony.[1]

We lived on a farm of 263 acres. I have heard my grandmother say that when they first went on to the farm, it seemed to be very poor, but by careful management it became quite productive. It was one of the handsomest farms I have ever seen, beautifully rolling with springs of clear soft water in abundance.

When they first occupied the farm, they lived in a log cabin, which was thought to be the first one ever built on the farm; but there were rose bushes, which were not wild roses, growing at another spot, which indicated that the first cabin was there. They lived in the old cabin but a few years, when they built another which was of hewed logs; that is, the logs were hewed on two sides. The spaces between the logs were "chinked" with bits of wood and then plastered with mortar so that it made a warm and comfortable room.

In 1795 my grandfather built a six room stone house adjoining the log one, using the latter as a kitchen. He built a large frame barn in the summer of 1816. I was four years old that April, but I remember the workmen hewing the timber, and doing a good many things about the barn; and I remember looking at a dead blue bird that some one had killed. My uncle, who inherited the farm [Mahlon K. Taylor, Jr.], built an addition of stone in place of the log kitchen, and some years after his death the whole was burned. When I was there last, there was nothing left but the stone spring house.

The kitchen of John's birthplace today. Courtesy of John G. Lewis, owner.

THE KITCHEN: CENTER OF THE HOME

The log kitchen was but one room, which was about twenty feet square; and it was used as long as I lived there as a kitchen, dining room and sitting room. A small bed room had been partitioned off in one corner.

In the evening, after the dishes were washed and cleared off the table and the table set back, the candle stand would be moved out from its proper corner and the whole family gathered around it; some of the men reading a newspaper or a book and the women sewing or knitting, or spinning flax or tow. If there was not room around the stand for all, one or more would hang a candle on the back of a chair. The candle sticks were tall iron sticks with a hook at the top by which they could be hung on the back of a chair. The sticks were so made that they would hold three or four inches of a candle, which could be raised up by a thumb piece. If the candle was hung on the second, instead of the top slat in the chair, it would sometimes burn a black stripe on the top one.[2] As long as my grandfather lived, until I was about eleven years old, he had a candle hung on the back of a chair for himself.

The kitchen chairs were common splint bottoms with slat backs, the splints from half to three quarters of an inch wide, and if a bottom gave out, we went into the woods, cut down a thrifty young white oak tree about three inches in diameter, split it into splints and mended or put a new bottom in the chair.

On the west side of the room was the fire place, which occupied nearly the whole side of the cabin. There was but room left for a winding "kitchen stairs" up to the kitchen loft, under which was the kitchen closet and in which the iron ware, pots, kettles, bake irons and such things were kept.

On the kitchen shelves were the table ware, including pewter plates and dishes, and mugs, the spoons lying in notches along the edge of a shelf.

Travelling tinkers were not strangers. They would come at frequent intervals and mend the tinware and remould the broken pewter spoons. Tin pedlars were common with a load of tin cups, buckets, coffee pots and such. The "earthern ware" including milk pans, pie dishes, pitchers, jars and jugs were bought at the store.

We had silver spoons, both table and tea, but they were not used by the family, only when visitors or strangers were present, and there was a china tea pot, sugar bowl, and teas to match, which were only used on special occasions. In every day use we had pewter spoons and dishes, among the dishes some platters twelve to fifteen inches in diameter.[3]

The whole fire place including the hearth was paved with large stone slabs which were hauled from a quarry five or six miles off. The fire was built with sticks or logs of woods four feet long. To build one, first put in a "backlog" six to twelve inches in diameter; then on a pair of heavy iron andirons (or "hand irons" as we had it) place against the backlog a "middle stick" about three or four inches in diameter; and then a forestick about six inches. Start the fire with some kindling and put in as many small sticks of wood as were deemed necessary. Chips from the woodpile made good kindling. And

>   "What matter how the North Wind roared—
>   Blow high, blow low, not all its snow
>   Could quench that hearth-fires ruddy glow."

Some people, for want of andirons, used stones large enough to keep the wood out of the ashes.

Our chimney was built of stone, but the pioneer chimney was usually built of wood above the fire place,[4] small sticks, and plastered with clay inside and out. They would last many years.

Our chimney was so large that you could sit at the end of the fire, and see the stars by looking up the chimney. On two iron bars, across the chimney, was placed an oak pole about two or three inches in diameter, called the "lug-pole." On this hung the pot-hooks and "trammels." These consisted of an iron bar about an inch and a half or two inches wide with a hook at the upper end large enough to hook over the lug-pole, and at the bottom a short piece bent at right angles with a hole punched through it. Similar holes were punched through the bar all the way up about two inches apart. A rod to fit the holes in the trammel bent at the top so as to enter the holes in the bar, [with] a hook at the bottom on which to hang a pot or kettle. By means of these holes in the trammel, a pot, kettle, or bake iron could be raised or lowered to suit the heat.

> When fireplaces supplied the heat, and candles the light, people heated and lighted only one room, except when company was coming. The whole family, including the help, tended to gather in the kitchen, where the fire had to be lit anyway. Despite the size of the wood used, a cooking fire in a kitchen fireplace would be considered small by today's standards. No flames roared up the chimney, lintel and lug-pole could be safely made of wood, and one might sit comfortably in one end of the fireplace while the fire burned in the other.
>
> James Russell Lowell knew how little heat a fireplace really supplied, even when well stocked with wood. In his poem "The Courtin'" an old Yankee, still unreconciled to new-fangled stoves, tells us:
> > A fireplace filled the room's one side
> > With half a cord o' wood in --
> > There warn't no stoves (tell comfort died)
> > To bake ye to a puddin'.

In some of the best cabins or kitchens, instead of a lug-pole, there was a crane, which was a heavy iron rod, set in two iron eyes fastened in the chimney jamb and having another rod fastened to the top of it so as to swing out over the fire, to which pots and kettles would be hung. They could be swung off the fire to be examined.

Iron pots and brass kettles were used in every kitchen.[5] Every family had a brass kettle for cooking fruit, making preserves and similar uses, and a large iron pot for boiling clothes on wash days. The "dinner-pot" was the one most used. It was of iron, to hold two or three gallons; and with a bail, to hang over the fire. Boiled dinners were very common; bacon and cabbage, "pickled pork" and cabbage, or salt beef and cabbage were favorite dinners and I remember them with a watery mouth. In the spring greens supplied the place of cabbage.

> By "greens" John does not mean such garden crops as kale, Swiss chard, spinach, lettuce, and collards. He is referring to plants that could be had in the fields for the taking, like tender polk shoots before they got tough and bitter, young mullein leaves, lambsquarter, water and field cress, and dandelions. The editors, a century after John, picked all these too, in fields only a mile or so away from the spots where his grandmother had sent him foraging. We did not, however, gather the sour dock that John mentions on page 36.

The "bake-iron" was a wrought iron slab about fifteen inches in diameter and half an inch thick, which had an iron handle on one side so bent and curved as to make the bake iron hang level over the fire. On it were baked buckwheat and corn cakes.

The "skillet" was cast, with three feet to stand on, a long handle cast on one side and a lid to fit the top, with a rim to hold coals on top. It was used for many purposes, cooking meat, baking biscuit, cooking hash and similar purposes. It was one of the most useful vessels about the kitchen. The stew pan has taken its place.

Frying pans were in use, differing from those now used only in the length of the iron handle. That was long enough to let the cook stand far enough from the fire for comfort, or to rest the handle on the back of a chair.

Another implement was the "spider," a small iron pot holding about three pints. It stood on three legs, usually long ones—whence its name—[6] and had a long handle, but usually no lid. It was used for cooking or heating small quantities of any thing.

A "gridiron" was an indispensable implement in every kitchen. It has been displaced by the broiler. It was cast and large enough to hold a fresh shad, and the broiling of salt shad was the main use. We did not have steak often enough to consider it a part of our diet.[7]

No kitchen was complete without a "dough-trough." This was a box four or five feet long, about two feet deep and the same width at the top, but narrower at the bottom, with a wide cover or "lid," which was used for making bread or pies on.

There was always a wooden "tray" in it, which was used for "mixing" bread, "working" butter and many other purposes. It was usually about two feet long by ten or twelve inches wide. It was worked out of a log like a canoe; but it has been superceded: first by the wooden bowl, turned by machinery out of a large tree, usually Buckeye, about two feet in diameter, and now that is superceded by the tin pan. There was also a rolling pin.

There was also a Dutch oven, which was a large cast iron pan; the common ones about a foot or fifteen inches in diameter and six inches deep. It stood on three legs, and had an ear cast on opposite sides by which it could be lifted or hung over the fire, and a cover with a raised rim. In this oven they could bake bread, biscuit or pies; or roast meat, by drawing some coals out in the hearth, and putting some on the lid.

One thing cooked in the Dutch oven will always be remembered by those who have eaten it, the "peach cobbler." Line the inside of the oven with pie crust, fill it with good ripe peaches, put on a top crust. And though there was a good deal of it, there was scarcely any left at the end of the meal.

> An insert, glued in, reads: "Miss Earle, in Old New York, says, 'A Dutch oven, or Dutch kitchen, was made of metal, usually tin, cylindrical in form, and open on one side, which was placed next the fire. Through this ran a spit by which meat could be turned while roasting.' That was known with us as a 'reflector.' Our 'Dutch oven' was a wholly different implement."
>
> The quotation is from *Colonial Days in Old New York*, by Alice Morse Earle, originally published in 1896, reprinted L.I., N.Y., 1962, page 122. Mrs. Earle (1853-1911) wrote 15 books and edited another. Of the 16, there were 13 in print in 1978—and one of them was on the lists of six separate publishers! John read several of her books, which bear such titles as *The Costume of Colonial Times, Child Life in Colonial Days,* and *Home Life in Colonial Days.*

We used the first "reflector" oven in the neighborhood. It was a tin box, open in front, and the other side so curved as to reflect the heat on to whatever was in it. There was a shelf and a dripping pan, and by placing the reflector close to a hot fire, a turkey or a roast or spare ribs could be roasted or biscuits baked.

We had the first cooking stove ever seen in the neighborhood, which the women soon learned to love. It took much less wood than the fireplace, did the cooking just as well, and with much less discomfort, but it had one discomfort for me. We had no means of starting a fire in the morning, if it had gone out during the night; and it was soon found out there was no person about the house could cover the fire in it to "keep" all night but myself, so I had to stay up till all were ready for bed. I have many times gone to a neighbor's house for fire in the morning, ours having gone out, and sometimes have gone to more than one before I could get it.

Those who had a shot gun could start a fire with it, but many of the farmers had no guns. With the old fashioned flint lock fire was easily started. "Prime" the gun, hold a bunch of tow to the pan, fire the gun (that is, "flash" it, for it must not be discharged) and the tow will be set on fire. We had no gun, until a young man living with us bought one.

I never heard of a tinder box until a stranger came with one in his pocket. It consisted of a gun flint, such as all guns had then, a small piece of steel and a bit of tinder. Hold a bit of the tinder on top of the flint between the thumb and finger, strike the edge of the flint with the steel, and the tinder would "catch fire."

Tinder was made of charred or scorched worn cotton or linen rags, preferably linen. "Punk" would also answer. We found it in hickory logs, where they had rotted with "dry rot." It would take fire from a spark.

The fire place was so large that the fire did not occupy more than half of it. After supper in winter nights the other part was usually filled by someone who had nothing to do, or something he could do there. It was a warm place to sit in.

Into it opened the mouth of the oven. In the best kitchens the bake oven opened along side the fire place so that the oven could be attended to without going out of doors. Ours was so.

Though the Taylor home is no longer in existence with its oven that made John proud, the Janney house where he was born is still in use as a residence and exhibits the same kind of oven. In both kitchens the mouth of the oven opened directly into the fireplace instead of out-of-doors. In the Janney house, now the home of Mr. and Mrs. John G. Lewis, you can still stand in the old fireplace and shovel hot coals into the oven.

The building of a bake-oven [out of doors] was a very simple process. Build a stone foundation of the right size and height and lay a floor of smooth stone, or bricks if bricks could be had, which was very rarely, and upon this floor build up a pile of dry wood the size and shape you wished the oven to be. Old rails were best, called "oven wood" because they were used to heat the oven in baking. And then plaster it over with mortar made of good clay, to the thickness of eight to twelve inches. A stone wall was built in front with a "mouth," through which the oven could be filled or emptied.

When the clay was fairly dry, fire was set to the wood, and a hole having been left in the rear of the oven to give it draft, the wood soon made a roaring fire which not only dried the clay, but burned it into a soft brick. Such an oven would last twenty or thirty years.

To clear out or fill the oven, an "oven peel" was used, which was a long handled wooden shovel, with which unburned coals and ashes could be shoveled out and then a large mop was used to clean the floor. Bread was sometimes baked on the oven floor.[8]

BAKING

Baking was always done on Saturday. The men must have provided ready on Saturday morning oven wood sufficient for the women. They would bake the oven full of bread and pies for the next weeks supply. The bread was made in large loaves, eight or ten or twelve inches in diameter and six inches thick.

The women made their own yeast (or "east" as we all called it) by fermentation of hops. Compressed yeast, not having been heard of, could not be bought at the store, as it can be now. Every garden had a hop vine in it and every housekeeper a hop bag. Baking powder had not been invented. Some used "salt rising," which we did not like. It made the bread have a peculiar taste, and if you were in a house where they were baking salt rising bread, it could be smelled in nearly all the house, and I never could think it a pleasant smell.

One good resulted from the weekly baking of bread. It should not be eaten until it is at least twenty four hours old, until it is "ripened." I have since known Virginians from the vicinity of Lynchburg, whose habit was to always have hot biscuits for breakfast and in order to have them and the coffee hot enough, the coffee pot would be left *on* the stove and the biscuit *in* it, during the meal.

We ate corn bread in several forms, from the pone, baked in the skillet, its full size: and about three inches thick, to the hoe cake, down to the batter cake.

At the time of butchering, we had "cracklin" bread. When the lard was rendered the leaf lard was kept separate, and the "cracklins" when the lard was fully cooked were kept. When broken into small pieces and mixed with corn bread before baking, with many people it added to the flavor of the bread.

> Of the foods just discussed, the days of salt-rising bread had already passed when the editors were boys. Instead, our mother had her own hop vine from which to make yeast, which we still called "east." Later on, she began buying compressed yeast—Fleischmann's—from the store. When we wanted the recipe for making salt-rising leaven, we had to look it up just now: a fermented mixture of salted milk, corn meal, flour, sugar, and baking soda.

> Cracklings from the lard pressing were still being mixed into corn bread to make crackling bread, though, and it was quite good, even if chiefly a way of getting around throwing out the cracklings. We ate the bread while it was hot, because if it was left standing, it got greasy.

> About lard: When customers brought lard in to our father's store to sell it, there were several things to be established. First, did it smell right, next was it "rusty" (discolored), and finally, was it all leaf lard, or just leaf lard poured on top? Leaf was choice lard, made from the fat around the hog's kidneys and the fat trimmed away from edible meat. Entrail, or caul, fat made a distinctly lower-grade product.

> Corn bread was baked in the oven in shallow, square pans. Hoe cakes had dropped from view, and "batter cakes" were a variety of pancake distinguished from "corn cakes" by being made of wheat flour, with no corn meal mixed in.

We also ate the corn "dodger" which was baked in cakes as large as the cook could mold in both hands, baked in the skillet. But what some thought was the best was the "hoecake." We did not bake it before the fire on a hoe but on the bake iron in a large cake about half or three quarters of an inch thick, and baked on both sides.

Much use was made of buckwheat. During the winter we had buckwheat cakes nearly every morning. We were fond of them, and the wheat brought the best price. Buckwheat cakes and molasses were a rarety [*i.e.* a delicacy]. At night the "batter-pot" was set near the fire to keep warm, and sometimes the batter would become too light. It was not an uncommon thing to find a good deal of the batter run over the hearth in the morning, and some crickets in the batter. Crickets were common in all kitchens. I have not seen a cricket for fifty years, except black ones.

> "The buckwheat
> Whitened broad acres, sweetening with its flowers
> The August wind."
>
> Bryant

Many used rye bread, which if properly made was good; but if not rightly made, was as one young housekeeper said of her first attempt, that she would as lieve have a ten pound cannon ball fired at her as that loaf of bread. Many used it because wheat brought the better price in the market.

> In those days the cash crop was wheat, and it was worth far more, comparatively, than it is today. A bushel of wheat would buy John's grandfather ten hours of work from a day laborer. Today a bushel is worth no more than an hour and a half's work.

Pop corn is not new. We used to parch the common corn, but pop-corn was not known in the neighborhood till about 1825.

Pancakes or slap-jacks were common. They were made of wheat batter fried in the frying pan, cooked on both sides. One test of the skill of the cook was, when a pancake needed turning, to take the handle of the frying pan, throw the cake into the air, and catch it the other side up.

Fritters (or "flitters") were rather a delicacy, made of rather stiffer dough and cooked in the same way as pancakes, but in small cakes. I rode with my mother (behind her) to see Aunt Pleasant and Aunt Jane, and I can not forget the fritters and wine sauce I ate.

A table was not properly set without pie. Apple pie was the standard, though from the time peaches were ripe until they were gone, they took the place of the apple, and as soon as pumpkins were ripe, they furnished the pies. In the winter, if the green apples were gone, we frequently had dried peach pie, and all else failing, dried apple pie. A dinner was hardly complete without some kind of pie, and it was frequently had at breakfast.

On rare occasions we had custard pie, precisely as we get it now.[9]

The fancy pie for weddings or such occasions was the potato pie. It was made by boiling the potatoes and passing them through a fine wire sieve, or "sifter" as we called it, and making the pie as they made the pumpkin pie, sometimes sweetened to taste.[10]

The pumpkin pies we ate were not flavored with spices of any kind, the only flavor they had came from the milk with which they were mixed. Johnson in his Wonder Working Providence says of the Pumpkin: "a fruit which the Lord fed his people with till corn and cattle increased."

> "We have pumpkins at morning and pumpkins at noon.
> If it were not for pumpkins we should be undone."[11]

According to Miss Earle, Higginson called them squanter-squashes; Josselyn squontorsquashes; Roger Williams askuta-squashes; and Wood isquoukersquashes;[12] and we have clipped it to squashes. The people of New England have no pumpkin pie, it is "squash" pie, and they used a kind that we thought unfit for pie, and knew as "cow pumpkins."

There were but two kinds of sugar, common brown New Orleans and loaf, the latter in conical loaves of about ten or twelve pounds always wrapped in strong, heavy paper of a dark purple color. We had no granulated, nor powdered sugar. Sugar and molasses always came in hogsheads, the former of about 1200 pounds and the latter of about 120 gallons. A store keeper in the country had to have his goods brought him in the wagons of his neighbors and the only way a hogshead of sugar or molasses could be unloaded was to take off the hind wheels of the wagon and let it down on the ground. A story was current that a Mr. Williams, an eccentric old man at Waterford, eight miles off, in unloading a hogshead of molasses, took the wheels off, letting the wagon down to within about a foot from the ground. The old man got a stiff plank to roll the hogshead down to the ground on, but was told it would surely break. He thought he knew better, but the moment the hogshead touched the plank, it broke, the hogshead fell to the ground, both heads bursted and the one hundred and twenty gallons of molasses ran into the gutter.

A note tipped in reads: "I have many times wondered where "hogshead" came from and now I have just learned from Brewer's Dictionary of Phrase & Fable that it comes from the Danish oxe-hud (ox-hide) which held about 260 Danish quarts while the goatskin held a smaller quantity."

We ate but few sweet cakes of any kind, sugar being a luxury. We would occasionally have some ginger cakes, sweetened, properly, with "Orleans" molasses. Some sweetened their coffee with it.

Some used roasted rye instead of coffee.

Candies were almost unknown. Stores did not keep them. The nearest point at which they could be had was at Leesburgh, eight miles off.[13]

MEATS

We ate very little fresh meat. About Christmas, when the fat hogs were killed for market, we would have the refuse: the livers, the hearts, the melts [*i.e.* the spleens], and, when those we intended for home use were cut up, the heads and feet; and when the hams were cut apart, we ate the part of the backbone between them, the "chine." That was generally eaten fresh, usually roasted, and if not too old and the skin properly scored, that is, cut into squares of about an inch, the skin was very crisp and the meat good.

The heads were thoroughly boiled so that the meat could be easily separated from the bones. With some other scraps, this was then chopped fine and put to press in the cheese press, and made into 'hogshead' cheese, which when properly seasoned (and ours was always so) we used to think a delicacy.

The scraps which came from trimming the hams, shoulders, and other pieces were made into sausages, for which purpose they must be thoroughly "chopped." We had no meat cutters such as the stores furnish now, but we had a chopping bench, a plank six or eight feet long set up on four legs, and narrow pieces nailed on all the sides so as to make a shallow box, into which the meat was put. With axes and hatchets the younger members of the family had the chopping to do. By the time we thought it was fine enough, the choppers were usually tired. My grandmother used to caution us not to chop it too fine or it would be poisonous; but when we became tired as we always did, and would ask if we might quit, she would say no, we need not be at all afraid. We at last concluded that she only meant that we could not chop it too fine.

Sausage making was a gala night with the family. While we were chopping the meat, the women were making preparations for the stuffing.

The cases, or to use the words we used, the "sausage guts," were the long small intestines, which would be, in the full grown hog, [more than fifteen feet long]. These were carefully saved while "ridding the guts"; that is, while cleaning them of the fat by which they were surrounded, and were put in brine and finally turned inside out, and by scraping cleaned of all mucus lining, leaving nothing but the thin and nearly transparent cuticle.[14]

The sausage stuffer was like a tin cup which would hold about a quart, with a conical bottom, to which was fastened a spout about an inch in diameter and about eight inches long and a plunger to fit it.

When the meat was chopped fine enough, it was removed to a tub or tray and seasoned with salt, pepper and pulverized sage leaves. Without sage sausage *was* not, and *should* not be made.

> John takes sides here in a controversy that was still raging in the neighborhood a century later: whether to use a heavy or a light hand while putting in the sage. The editors and—especially—their mother were Little Sage-ians.

When properly tempered, as a mason would say of his mortar, the stuffer was filled with the meat, and a skin slipped over the end of the nozzle. Some one taking the stuffer in both hands applied the handle of the plunger to his breast, and forced the sausage into the skin. Now, sausage skins are imported from Italy by the keg or barrel, including hog, beef, and sheep big and little.

We would then have sausage as long as it lasted. Sometimes some of it was packed away in a stone jar [*i.e.* a stoneware jar] and melted lard poured over it so as to fill all the interstices, and it would keep sweet a long time. Some tried to preserve it by smoking but I never thought it fit to eat.

We also had pigs feet. The feet were cut off close up to the ham, or at the knee of the fore leg; and were eaten fresh when thoroughly boiled. They were afterwards fried. Some "soused" them; pickled them in brine and vinegar.

Spare ribs were a delicacy. In making "clear sides" for market or[15] for smoked bacon all the ribs were cut out. In a second grade, the butt end of the ribs was left in. The ribs cut out were the "spare" ribs, and were eaten fried, or roasted by hanging them before a hot fire by a twisted string, by which they were kept turning as by a spit (which we did not have). In this way the ribs could be delicately roasted.

A pudding set under the ribs in a "dripping" or "bake" pan on some hot coals, so that the dripping from the ribs should drop on it, was, as were the ribs, delicious.

We always smoked some hams, shoulders and sides of the hogs slaughtered and ate them, fried or boiled.[16]

We would occasionally kill a bull calf but rarely, for it was more profitable to raise them [as steers], and always kept the heifers. In some neighborhoods, when a calf was killed, three of the quarters were distributed among three of the neighbors, who would return the loan when they killed a calf, thus giving them all fresh meat oftener. We simply "killed" a calf, but we "butchered" a beef or a hog.

Once a year, in the late fall, we would fatten and butcher a steer, or sometimes an old worn out cow; then we would have meat for a short time. The head and shanks were boiled until the meat could be easily seperated from the bones; it was then chopped as sausage meat, and made into mince pies. Mince meat for sale was not known.[17]

There was little or no use made of mutton.

We made free use of chickens: roasted, fried, "smothered," chicken pie or "pot pie," and on state occasions a roast turkey, or goose.

During the summer we ate salt meat or salt fish daily. We always had a barrel of salt, fat "pickled" pork. This or bacon was eaten boiled with cabbage, or greens.

There was also a barrel of salt beef which was eaten in the same way; and there is no dinner that can be set before me now which I enjoy more than one of corned beef and cabbage, *if well cooked.* I am glad to learn that President Roosevelt agrees with me, or properly, I agree with him.[18]

In the spring, a load of flour was always hauled to Alexandria and some shad bought. They usually cost about four dollars per hundred. We would then have fresh shad as long as they would keep fresh, and we had a barrel of salt ones for summer use. Salted and broiled shad was a standard breakfast all summer. At night one would be taken to the spring house and put in the "drain," where a stream of fresh water would run over it all night, and in the morning it would be nearly fresh.

We did not eat herrings, though many of the neighbors did. It was not at all uncommon to see, near the back door of a kitchen some herrings with a stick run through the gills, hung up to dry after having been soaked in fresh water. In the lower counties of Virginia, and Maryland, herrings were eaten instead of shad, costing much less. The tradition in our neighborhood was that if you could get at the naked skin of one of the people from that section, you could feel the herring bones sticking out.

Farmers did not have bells to ring for meals as they now have, but they had either a tin "dinner horn" or a conch shell with the point cut off, which made a capital trumpet. Nearly all farmers had an eight day clock in a tall case, which occupied a prominent place in the front hall or the parlor; others had cheaper ones, fastened to the wall without any case. Many of them had also a "noon mark." As accurately as they could, they would make a mark on the floor at the south door, or on the porch, which, when touched by the shadow of the door jamb or a post, would show noon. I have listened with great interest many a day for the sound of that horn.

We had no "fly papers" such as are now used but we had fly traps. One was a glass tumbler filled nearly full of soap suds, with a slice of bread with a hole in the center and the under side covered with molasses, and laid in the tumbler.

Another was two shingles tied together at the thick end, hung up by a string and smeared with molasses. When covered with flies, clap them together. Both were effective.[19]

GOING TO MARKET

The nearest cities and the nearest ports for the export of agricultural products were Georgetown and Alexandria, Virginia, and so these naturally formed the chief markets that supplied Loudoun farmers with what cash they got.

When we went to Alexandria or Georgetown with a load of flour or pork, we took our own feed for horses and drivers. We had but a four horse team. Many of the farmers had six horses. Our wagon would "bed" twelve barrels of flour, that is, six couples laid end to end would just cover the bottom of the wagon. If the roads were good, two more barrels would be placed on top of the others. Flour was packed in barrels holding one hundred and ninety six pounds of flour each. It was never packed in sacks as it is now. The load was put in and then "rye chop," rye straw cut in a cutting box into about inch pieces, mixed with ground rye; and hay, with a little corn—enough for the whole trip, which took about a week.[20] The wagon was covered with a white cotton wagon cover stretched over the bows which left room over the load for a good deal of hay. There was a "wagon trough" hung to the hind end of the wagon which could be fastened on the top of the tongue. In the wagon trough was carried the wagon bucket, a large wooden bucket to water the horses during the day, and the tongue prop, to support the tongue while the horses were being fed. The wagon tongue was fastened stiff in the hounds [the bars that connected tongue and front-wheel assembly] and would not fall to the ground as they do now.[21]

At night the horses were unhitched and the "gear" [harness] taken off and hung on rails or poles run between the spokes of the hind wheels, the horses hitched to the trough and fed. If the road was muddy, as soon as the horses were dry they were thoroughly curried, but they stood at the wagon all night, no matter what the weather.

We had our own bed, made of heavy spreads, or "quilts," wide enough for two which were carried rolled tight and tied with straps or cords; and our "dinner box," in which was enough to eat for the whole trip.

After the horses were cared for, the landlord gave us room on the floor for our beds, fire if needed, a table on which we could spread our supper, and a pot of coffee. In the morning we had coffee for breakfast, and we paid for the coffee and a small room rent, which was all the pay he got except for an occasional meal and the sale of some hay or feed when a wagoner was out, and the liquor he sold, of which many of the wagoners drank freely.

There were several drovers' rests along the road. The Dranesville Tavern, for instance, was advantageously located for travelers from the west, near the junction of the Falls Road to Georgetown with the Leesburg Pike to Alexandria. Since John's grandfather and uncles took most of a week to make the trip from the farm, they obviously had hard going and spent a night or so at their destination, perhaps with relatives. Later, however, after the roads had been improved, John's Uncle Mahlon, with a helper or so, could make the tavern in

one long day's driving, stay overnight, leave very early the next
morning, transact his business in either Georgetown or Alexandria,
and get back to the tavern's cold comfort by nightfall. The evening of
the third day would see him home again. The old tavern still stands
beside State Route 7.

There were nearly always two or more teams together on the road;
many times half a dozen. I have seen twelve teams, nearly all of them "six
horse," in a string: and if one of them got stalled, as was not infrequent,
for the roads were wholly unimproved, the rest would help him out.
Anyone who has ever traveled over Tramel's hill or Gordon's lane will
remember it.

Our house was close to the "big road" which ran from Snickersville
[Bluemont] to Leesburgh being part of the main highway between the
Shenandoah valley and Washington and Alexandria and over which was
hauled nearly all the flour from the Valley to market. Six horse or four
horse teams were nearly always in sight going or returning. I once saw a
line of twelve six horse and four horse teams going as close together as
they could all loaded with flour for Alexandria. After the railroad was
completed to Winchester, there was not one team a week passing and if
one did pass it belonged to a neighboring farmer. It took away a good deal
of the life of those living on that road.[22]

The drop in traffic along the Leesburg Pike developed in the
decades after John left Loudoun but before the Civil War, as the
railroad from Winchester to Harpers Ferry took over the work of
hauling to market the wheat and flour of the Valley of Virginia.
After the War, the Pike received its coup de grace from the
Washington and Old Dominion Railroad, which in 1874 reached
Bluemont and offered Loudouners an easy way to get their hay, beef,
eggs, and chickens to Washington and Alexandria.

Oversets were not at all uncommon. Near our house the road had
worn a gulley, nearly deep enough to hide a wagon. A driver was walking
along the bank, and his saddle horse holding back on his breast chains,
while the off horse did not, threw the wheels out of the track, and up the
bank, until the wagon upset, and they had to unload and reload it.

My uncle went to Baltimore to haul back a load of goods. There were
two other teams along. One of them was driven by a drunken fellow, who

was hardly ever sober. Rain had made the roads very slippery, and as I walked along behind his wagon, I saw the driver open his "wagon box," take out his bottle and take a long pull at it. In his attempt to put it back in the box, he dropped it in the track and the hind wheel ran over it. Every teamster kept a stone quart bottle of whiskey in his wagon box, with his curry comb and brush.

A few minutes afterwards, the driver having got a little out of the track, the hind wheels began to slide over towards the gutter, and before my voice could reach him, the wagon, loaded to the bows with store goods, laid flat in the gulley. All came to his help, and with a good many left-handed blessings, unloaded and reloaded the goods.

About Christmas, the hogs intended for market, which had been put in a pen in the early winter to fatten, were butchered. We had no such appliances as they have in the stockyards of today. We brought our big sled into the lower part of the yard near the spring and fastened it to the ground so that it would not move, and dug a hole so that we could lean a hogshead against the hind end of the sled, and fill it with water. Upon a large fire of wood which would make a hot one, we would place a lot of boulders which would stand fire, not flint nor slate, for they would split to pieces. When they became hot they were plunged into the water in the hogshead. We would then "stick" a hog, and when it was fully bled, plunge it into the hot water, and soon have it clean and on the gallows.

The business of the women was to "rid the guts," that is to strip off the fat by which they were covered. In doing this they would lay aside the sausage skins, and some times they would cut or tear a gut, and that would cause trouble. The hogs were left hanging all night and the next day were loaded into the wagon and taken to market at Alexandria or Georgetown.

FOODS

We used to lay in on that trip salt, both coarse and fine, enough to last a year, and common New Orleans sugar. We had three kinds of salt: coarse or alum or Turks Island; common; and fine or ground alum. The alum came in large hard grains like pulverized alum.[23]

We also always bought four or five bushels of oysters, which we would keep till used by piling them on the cellar floor, and when we saw any of them opening, sprinkle them well with brine. They would close with a snap.

Miss Earle reports a writer as eating Gowanus oysters "some of them

The garden yielded its plenty

not less than a foot long."[24] The unwritten law of Lower Maryland and Virginia could not have prevailed there, for that forbids the cutting of an oyster in two, you must eat them whole.

We used to roast them on the kitchen fire till they opened. Our method was to lay two sticks of wood about an inch apart on a good bed of hot coals, and lay the oysters on their backs, so that they would not lose any juice and then we had oysters fit "for a queen." We got the delicious juice which is lost in the oyster that has been shucked. The canned oyster had not been invented.

> George III and George IV were the British monarchs of John's years in Loudoun, and when he died, Edward VII occupied the throne. Victoria, however, ruled the Empire during most of his life and would have sprung instantly to anyone's mind who thought of a monarch, so that "fit for a queen" came easily to John's pen.

We made but little use of soups. We occasionally had dumplings, which were simply pie dough cut into diamonds and thoroughly cooked. Occasionally, we had noodle soup, which we understood to be a pioneer dish. It was made of pie dough cut into narrow strips and thoroughly cooked in a soup, of which my recollection is rather pleasant. It was called a German dish. Occasionally we had chicken soup. Of soups proper we knew nothing.

We used hominy very freely during the winter. We could not buy it as we can now, but had to "pound" it for ourselves. Every neighborhood, but not every farm had a hominy mortar. We would take an oak log, about four or five feet long, and a foot or fifteen inches in diameter, and by cutting, boring and burning would excavate a bowl in one end that would hold a peck or more of corn. We would fasten an iron wedge, that we used to split rails with, into the end of a handle to use as a pestle or pounder, put about two quarts of smooth, hard grained "flint" corn in the mortar, pour in hot water enough to soften the hulls of the corn, and pound it lightly, so as not to break the grains, until the hulls were loose, and we had a good hominy, which we ate boiled and fried after it got cold. Hominy mills had not been invented.

My uncle, on an adjoining farm, fastened a "spring-pole" overhead in the shop, [from] the end of which the pestle or "beater" was suspended, and it made the work of pounding much easier.

Pounding hominy was an evening job. If the men were notified that some was needed, they would on one evening select and shell half a bushel or a bushel of corn, and the next evening carry it to the mortar and pound it. We never took daylight to do it in.

It was eaten boiled, or with milk as we ate mush and milk, or when it was cold, fried for breakfast.

Milk was a standard food. We used it at all times and in all ways, but we got only "skim-milk."[25] Mush and milk was on almost every supper table, and in the morning, the cold mush left at supper was cut into lumps like loaf sugar and put into a pot of boiling milk. When the mush had become warmed through, it was eaten for breakfast; and I remember it with a watery mouth. Most cooks do not know how to make mush. They do not boil it enough. Corn cannot be spoiled by over cooking. One old aunt who was known among her friends as making uncommonly good mush said she always boiled it two hours.

Mush was also fried for breakfast. We occasionally had our supper varied by rye mush which was liked by nearly all.

Of potatoes, beets, turnips, parsnips ("pasnips") and cabbages we had abundance, but of the modern method of eating cabbage raw or as slaw we knew nothing.

The safest and best way to preserve vegetables was to bury them in a pit. They would come out in the spring fresh and crisp; but with cabbage it was wise before using to strip off all the loose leaves, or you might find a "fishing worm" or a "sow bug," or as the entomologists call it, "an air-breathing ovacoid isopod," on the dinner table.

We had two kinds of potatoes, "red" and "white," both "Irish." During my boyhood the Mercer or Neshamock was introduced, and it was very good, none better now. We boiled or roasted them, the latter preferred as long as the fireplace was used, when they were roasted in the ashes.

> Dr. Raymond Webb, of the Vegetable Laboratory of Beltsville Agricultural Center, has no record of the Mercer, or Neshamock, potato, but says that is not surprising. Between 1800 and 1900, private growers developed potatoes with perhaps 150 different names, though sometimes, as here, the same strain might bear different names, depending on who offered the seed potatoes for sale.

We had but two kinds of corn, yellow and white, with small, round hard grains and a big cob, such as farmers will not plant at all now.

We always grew some sweet potatoes, that were good though not equal to those from farther south as I have since learned, but we never ate, nor saw any but our own growing.

We sometimes pulled up our cabbages and kept them in the cellar. The old cabbage stalks and turnips left over were frequently made use of by planting them in the spring. The stalks would produce a good crop of sprouts, which made delicious greens, but our main dependence for greens was dandelions and sour dock. We had never heard of such a thing as cultivated greens. An improved dandelion is now (1901) cultivated for greens.

Every family put up a supply of pickles. They had no such cucumbers as are now grown especially for pickles but they pickled those they grew when of the proper size, and salted them in an oak barrel, and when needed soaked the salt out and put them in vinegar. They pickled green beans, which many preferred to cucumbers. Some pickled green walnuts, butternuts (white walnuts) if they could be had.[26]

NUTS AND FRUITS

The boys always laid in a supply of walnuts to be cracked and eaten on winter evenings. There were a few hazel nuts to be got along the fence rows, and a few hickory nuts in the woods, but no chestnuts.

We had no cultivated grapes or berries, except gooseberries, and they were very poor.

> The lack of chestnuts was not due to the blight, which would not strike for nearly a century. Plenty of chestnut trees grew on the Blue Ridge, eight miles off, and as late as 1920 families were still organizing

Sunday outings to gather the nuts. Among the berries should be included the currants that John mentions later on.

Blackberries and dewberries were plentiful, the former along the fence rows and the latter in the open fields. I have a distinct remembrance of having the briars rake across my naked instep in the harvest field. I never saw a cultivated strawberry or blackberry until I was thirty years old,[27] nor a cultivated grape. There were no strawberries nor plants for sale, no grapes nor grape vines, nor peach trees. I never heard of selling an apple nor a peach, nor a flower.

During the fall and winter we had apples in plenty. We ate them raw, in pies and sauce, roasted or baked, [and] cut in slices across the apple and fried in butter. But I never saw an uncooked apple at the table. They were not considered food but were eaten at odd times, after supper or whenever they happened to be in sight.

We had an orchard of seven acres, but there were not more than a dozen trees which bore fruit worth anything. There were about half a dozen Newtown Pippins, not now excelled by any winter apple, one early sweet bough, one Vanderver, and one Spitzbergen. The rest were all seedlings, but one of which bore good fruit. I picked from one tree sixty three bushels of Newtown pippins, all perfect apples, letting the imperfect ones fall to the ground, the largest crop I ever heard of, and the editor of Meehans Monthly said the same.

Benjamin Franklin exhibited the Newtown Pippin in London in 1759. The apple originated on Long Island, but is known today also as the Virginia, or Albemarle, Pippin. It has a yellowish color. Several apples bear Vandevere in their names, the plain Vandevere being marked with red streaks over a yellow background, becoming deep red. Esopus Vandevere, an old apple that may have originated in Colonial days, is still around but not much grown for market. These are all "snappy" eaters, good for cooking and keeping. (From a letter from Larry L. McGraw, who is keeping old varieties of fruit alive at his Experimental Garden, Portland, Oregon.) In *Apples of New York*, S.A. Beach says of the Sweet Bough that "as a kitchen fruit in its honied sweetness and tender flesh, it has no equal of its season," which extends from late July through August. It is greenish-yellow to yellowish-white, and not widely grown today, since it is too soft for shipping.

In the fall, when the apples were ripe, we would get the big road wagon bed full, take them to the cider press, two of which were within three miles of us, and make cider, which we would use as long as we could keep it sweet, and let the rest go to vinegar.

Once my grandmother and my mother were very much annoyed by finding the vinegar full of wriggling "little eels." They thought the vinegar spoiled, though it seemed very good. They tried to strain the eels out by thick flannel, they tried boiling it, but all tricks failed to get shut of them, and they had to give it up, and let the eels live. None of us understood it. Now nearly all school children understand it.

> A hundred years later vinegar eels were an accepted part of vinegar making, and we simply lived with them. They are little nematode worms.

My uncle and I concluded one fall, when we had several barrels of good cider, to try an experiment. When the cider had worked so as to clear itself, we put two gallons of rye whiskey (we had not learned how to make whiskey out of corn) into a clean 32-gallon barrel and racked off enough of the clear cider to fill the barrel. The whiskey checked the fermentation, but when it was two years old it became a very seductive drink, for it was pleasant to the taste, and a tumbler full of it could be sensibly felt. My grandmother had just enough of mischief in her, to make her play the cider off on a caller once in a while. Uncle Bernard Taylor, a plain old Friend who sat at the head of our meeting, was noted for his joyous, jovial disposition. Whenever he knew of a gathering of women, at a quilting for instance, he would find his way there. One day, he called at our house on his way to a quilting at a neighbors, and my grandmother, knowing his fondness for good cider, offered him a glass, which he praised highly. When he left, she asked him if he would like another glass. "Yes, he would." She gave him another and he rode off. The women reported that they had never seen him so merry as he was that day. He kept them in an uproar for an hour after he got there. My grandmother enjoyed their story, as one after another of them told it as she met them.

> As a "plain Friend," Uncle Bernard would have used the plain language of Quakers, including *thee* and *thy* for *you* and *your*, and would have worn the plain dress, which at that time included knee britches. Since he "sat at the head of meeting," he had a special

function: A meeting for worship is supposed to end not because a set time has arrived but because—well, because it has *ended*.

Bernard Taylor would have sat at the end of a facing bench("at the head of meeting") and been the one who decided that the end had indeed arrived. He would have signaled the fact by shaking hands with the person sitting next to him, whereupon a general shaking of hands throughout the room would have ensued. Then, after some long, neighborly chats, Friends would have gone home.

The women usually made some home-made beer during the summer, and I remember drinking it; but have forgotten how it was made.[28]

We dried apples and peaches, the apples from some which ripened early but were too sour for any other use, and were not improved by drying. My uncle took some dried peaches to Georgetown, which were carefully dried in the sun and from good ripe fruit, but he could not sell them at all at any price, because they had not been peeled.

There were no peach orchards. The peach trees grew along the fence rows (some of them planted, but nearly all volunteer), and in or by old stumps in the fields.

There was a distillery in almost every neighborhood, and many farmers took their apples and peaches there, and had them turned into apple and peach brandy.

There was but one pear tree in the neighborhood which bore edible pears, and the boys of the neighborhood got a good share of them. As an illustration of their conduct one young man took off his trousers, tied strings around the bottom of the legs, filled them with pears, and carried them home. The tree stood in a field where a cabin once was, and the owner placed his big road wagon under the tree with two of his boys in it as watchmen. They fell asleep and some others ran the wagon down the hill and upset it in a spring branch, their comrades stoning the wagon so as to keep them in it from escape. The old man became so vexed that he cut the tree down.

There were some seedling trees on our farm which bore a good looking pear, but we thought a pear, like an apple, got ripe in the tree, and they never got ripe, as we thought.

John's family had not learned to pick home-grown pears from the tree before they fell, wrap them in paper, and store them for several weeks.

JOHN'S BEDROOM

My bed room, during nearly all the time after I left my mother's arms till I was twenty years old, was in the kitchen loft. It was large enough for a large "colonial chest" and three beds, and still room for the flour barrel, the corn meal, the buckwheat meal, and the salt barrel, besides the "big wheel" (the wool wheel), the "little wheel" (the flax wheel), the reel, and the rats.

There were always two beds in the room, one occupied by my uncle and a farm hand, the other by Bill Shuy and myself. Bill was so near an idiot that he never learned to do any work on the farm except to cover corn at corn planting, carry sheaves at harvest, and rake after a cradler. He could not bind [sheaves]. He could feed and milk the cows, and slop the hogs, but never could learn his letters nor count his fingers.

He was an illustration of the kindness of the family. My grandfather, wishing to take a boy to "raise," went to the poor house to get one. They let him have Billy, and he took him home behind him on his horse. On his way home, he thought the boy talked rather silly, and they soon found he was an idiot: but the sympathies of all the family were so aroused for him that they concluded to keep him. At the time of my grandfather's death, Bill was over thirty years old: but my uncle, who inherited the farm, kept him. At his death, the children concluded to and did send Bill back to the poor house; but the sympathy of two of them, a brother and sister, was so alive, that they took Bill out of the poor house, took him to their home where they had no possible use for him; and kept him, fed him, and clothed him until his death.

Our bed room, during the half of my life there, had but one window, a four pane of seven by nine glass and could not be opened. Afterwards there was a dormer window put in the roof. The roof was so low that when my bed was pushed out close to the side of the room, I have frequently bumped my head against the rafters getting in or out of bed. With no ventilation and the heated roof only two or three feet off, in the summer it was a hot bed room, but in the winter it was cool enough. The gable end was "weather boarded," not with jointed narrow siding such as is now used, but with oak, as wide as the log would make, and they were so warped that the wind and snow came in freely. When our bed was in the west end of the room, I have frequently felt the snow falling in my face and the wind blow the hair about my head, but I never slept better in any bed room than in that kitchen loft.

When sawed with an up-and-down saw, in a water-operated mill, planks were made as wide as possible to save running them through the saw again. Since it would have been virgin timber, some pretty wide boards resulted that could warp badly.

There was one drawback. The rats had control under the kitchen floor, and climbed up the chimney well into the loft. Sometimes just as we were going to sleep, one would commence on a flour or meal barrel to gnaw his way in, and we would throw our shoes (we did not wear boots) at him and frighten him off. If we could find old Blacky or Browney and take her to bed with us, she would keep the rats quiet.

I woke one morning with my hand and bed clothes "muddy," for which I was wholly unable to account until I worked my hand, when the mark of a rat's teeth were very plain, and the scar is still plain.

Bill woke one morning with his face and pillow bloody. He did not know what was the matter until he washed his face, when it was found that a rat had bit him on the end of the nose. I have seen them make such bites. They will look intently at their object, when their lips will be drawn back, their jaws begin to play very rapidly, and with a sudden nip, they will run for their holes. No bad results follow. In the cases mentioned, neither of us would have known that we were bitten but for the blood and the little scar left.

No one shot the little screech owl

BIRDS

The worst fright I ever had was, as I lay in bed one night. It was very hot: and I was lying uncovered. I was aroused by a frightful noise on the roof not more than three feet above my head. It seemed to me something was tearing the roof off. The noise ceased for a moment and was followed by the most unearthly gutteral hoo-hoo-hoo I ever heard. I have laughed many times when I have remembered that as soon as I could muster courage enough, I pulled the sheet over myself as a protection. I was told in the morning that what I heard was an owl. Several years afterwards as I was passing through the woods I startled an owl, and as it flew it uttered the sound that I remembered so well. It was not the common hoot, that was familiar, but hoo, hoo, hoo, hoo, in a hoarse rattling sound which seemed to come out of the ground.

Two kinds of owl were common, what we knew as the "Big Owl," which is known by ornithologists as the Strix Nebulosa, or Barred Owl, and the pretty little Screech Owl. The te-whit-hoo-hoo-hoooh of the former could be heard any summer evening in the woods, and the quavering whistle of the latter about the barn or the house. The "Big Owl" was fair game for any body's gun, but the Screech Owl was not injured.

Birds were abundant: robins, quails ("partridges"),[29] sparrows (especially the "Chipping bird"), common crows, hawks of several kinds, turkey buzzards in flocks, black birds (both Crow and swamp, or red-winged), Jay birds, wrens, king birds, pewees, barn and chimney swallows, Orioles, mocking birds, cat birds, meadow larks, cow buntings, woodpeckers (of nearly all sorts, from the great Ivory-billed down to the smallest), snipes, Jack and great or wood cock, an occasional eagle, whippoorwill, martins, and little blue herons, known as "shite pokes." In the spring and fall large flocks of wild geese and ducks would fly over on their way north or south. Occasionally, in a foggy morning, when they failed to see their way, a flock would alight. Of the whole list I can recall but three which were not liable to be shot by any one who could get the use of a gun: the two swallows and the oriole. Two I have always missed in Ohio: the Baltimore Oriole and the Chattering, or House Wren.

> You will have noticed that the house, or English, sparrow and the starling were unknown to John's boyhood. The one did not come over from Europe till 1853, and the other till 1890. The English sparrow, which thrives on the grain it finds in horse food and horse manure, was ubiquitous in the editors' youth, but its numbers have tapered off, though the starling thrives.

In the fall when acorns were ripe, immense flocks of the wild, or Passenger Pigeon would make their appearance, so large as to cover the whole farm, of two hundred and sixty three acres. Flocks a mile across would obscure the sky: but now a wild pigeon can not be found.

The method of catching them has disappeared with the pigeons. We would select a high point in a field to set our net. The net was knit of strong twine, spun and twisted by the women, with meshes one and a half or two inches wide, the net twenty to forty feet long, and ten or twelve feet wide. Attach a good half inch rope twenty or thirty feet long, to two opposite corners, lengthwise of the net. We would cut limbs well supplied with leaves and build a "bough-house" to hide us from the pigeons. In this bough-house we would drive securely so as to stand firmly, a tough green stake to which one of the ropes of the net would be fastened.

At a proper distance, out in the field we would drive a similar stake, to which the other rope would be fastened, so as to stretch the net its full length. The other edge of the net was fastened, at the corners to pegs driven into the ground so that when the net was "sprung," it would open out its full size.

The tough green stakes, when bent down and fastened, supplied the force to jerk the long ropes and whip the net up and over the pigeons when suddenly released.

Then a proper arrangement was made by which the net could be "set," that is, it could be fastened down so as to occupy but about a foot between the two edges of the net.

A pigeon would be blindfolded, that is, its eyes would be sewn together by a fine needle and fine thread. It would be placed on a "stool," an apparatus by which, by pulling a cord it could be raised about a foot and suddenly let fall, when it would flutter as though it was just lighting on the ground. Another pigeon would be blinded in the same way, cloth boots fastened on its legs, and a twine forty or fifty feet long fastened by one end to a peg in the ground, and the other end to the "flyer's" legs. The net "set" and its "bed" well supplied with corn or acorns, and we were ready for a flock.

As soon as one appeared, we all hid in the bough-house. If the flock was flying very high we knew it would not stop, but if it was flying low, but little above the tree tops, when it came near, we would throw up a flyer which would fly to the length of its string, and then come to the ground. If the flock checked its flight, we would play the stool pigeon, and the flock would light on the corn and go to eating ravenously. As soon as all or nearly all of them were on the net, by a sudden pull on the rope the net would be sprung, and sometimes we could catch the whole flock.

The pigeons, in their efforts to escape would thrust their heads through the meshes, and we would go over the net, take a pigeons head between forefinger and thumb, and crush the skull. Cruel! I hear from a pretty girl with an Egret feather in her hat. Yes it was cruel, had we caught the pigeons purely for our amusement, but we ate them, while she hires some miscreant to skin the living Egret that she may wear its feathers in her hat. She has no right to complain or criticize even the Englishman who, on going out one morning said to his friend What a delightful morning, Tom. Let's go out and kill something.

We caught from one to twelve dozen at a haul, and in one day one hundred and forty four dozen. They were usually not tender, as caught, but if fed a few weeks, they made an excellent pot pie. Teamsters, on their way to market took them by sacks full, or "bags" full, for we had no "sacks" then.

HUNTING AND FISHING

Quails or "partridges" were plenty, but we knew nothing about shooting them on the wing but we tracked them to the roosting or "huddling" place.

By finding the track of a flock in the snow in the early morning and following it carefully we could always find them huddled in a bunch with their heads all pointing outward in a ring. A young man on the farm once found a flock huddled and fired at it, killing all but one. He killed twenty three.

Some caught them with nets. A partridge net was made of the same material as a pigeon net but was cylindrical, eighteen inches to two feet in diameter, on hoops, and twelve or fifteen feet long, with two wings twenty or more feet long and almost two feet wide, supported by stakes by which they could be kept upright. Set the wings, extending out at an angle from each side of the net and then "drive" the quails and they would follow the wings into the net.[30]

The amusements of my childhood were meager and consisted mainly in wading in the "run" and watching the minnows of which there were always plenty but very rarely a fish large enough to eat. The "run," as we called it was the head of one of the main branches of Goose Creek. It took its rise in a spring on an adjoining farm, but a summer rarely passed without its being turned into a roaring torrent that washed the fences away that crossed it.

I can recall the many happy hours I have spent along its grassy banks watching the little fish scooping out their nests. The "chub" was the largest fish I ever saw there, except on rare occasions, a sucker. The chub was I presume what the naturalists call the Cut-lips, Day Chub: Nigger Chub; and is known as a boys fish because it takes the bait quickly. It sometimes grew to six inches in length.

> The appellation "nigger" was rapidly dying out when the editors were boys, but a century earlier John would have grown up knowing blacks mostly as slaves — and if not as slaves, then as freemen whose feelings didn't have to be worried about much.

Occasionally a sucker might be seen, but I am unable to identify it. The only one described that fits it at all is the "Common Sucker": the White Sucker: Brook Sucker: Fine-scaled Sucker. The authorities say "it bites at a small hook baited with a worm," but the sucker of my boyhood could not be induced to bite at anything. Its mouth ended in a snout that was turned downwards and I think was never closed. The only way to catch it with a hook was to "hook" it: which was done by dropping a naked hook so as to catch in its mouth. It was not often that one large enough to be worth catching came into the run, but I have tried to coax them to bite, but always failed.

Eels would occasionally find their way. Once, when a cousin and I were using our handkerchiefs for a net to catch minnows we caught a young eel about six inches long.

> A hundred years later, Loudoun boys were still catching minnows with handkerchiefs. One simply laid his handkerchief on the bottom of the branch, weighting the edges with little stones. The minnows at once formed a school over it, whereupon one gathered up the handkerchief and poured the minnows into a lard can half full of water. The next day one emptied out the water and the dead minnows, which had expired as the oxygen in the water got used up.

There were but few fish in the streams, none which could be caught with a hook but cat fish, and an occasional sun fish or eel. We used birds for bait. By going to a mill dam three miles off, if we got there by day break, when the cat fish were going back from the creek to deep water in the dam, we usually caught a good mess of small fish, rarely more than eight or nine inches long.

Katoctin creek, at the nearest point one mile from our house, had a few cat fish and eels.[31] At night we would "gig" eels. An eel-gig was an iron fork, with three or four barbed prongs two or three inches long, the barbs pointing upward to prevent the eel from slipping off when struck. The gig was fastened to a slender handle about six feet long. The fisherman would take the gig in one hand and a bundle of "lightwood" in the other, made of dry shingles from an old roof or the bark from a shell-bark hickory, and wade quietly in the creek. If we saw an eel or a fish, and were quick enough, we could strike it with the gig. We would follow the creek down to the mill dam, about three and a half miles from home making a tramp of about seven miles, for three or four or perhaps half a dozen eels, some of them two feet or thirty inches in length.

Rabbits or hares were plenty and with a good dog were thought to be sport. When a light snow had fallen then boys thought it sport to track them and we caught them with snares.[32]

"Coon" and "Possum" hunting were favorite sports with many. A good "Coon-dog" was a favorite. A party would ramble all over the woods at night with their dogs and axes, and if a coon was treed, the tree was cut down.

There were no foxes in our neighborhood, but four or five miles off there were fox hounds, whose rather mournful yelp we could often hear.

THE GARDEN

My grandmothers garden was large enough to grow a full supply of garden vegetables. In three of the four corners stood a quince tree. Quinces were used mainly for preserves, of which we always had a large supply; including quinces, peaches, cherries, plums and watermelon rhinds. Quinces were also dried and used to give flavor to apple sauce.

On one side of the garden was a row of currant bushes. Currants were used before ripe for pies, which, at that time in the year were always highly prized; and when ripe, they were used for jelly. Almost every family in the neighborhood made a keg of currant wine every year; which was used in case of sickness, or on special occasions.

Along two sides of the garden were several damson plum trees which bore full every year, and the plums were used largely for preserves. There were two trees of a different kind, but the curculio [a plum weevil], which never troubled the damsons never allowed one of the other kind to get ripe. We never heard the name of the "Little Turk," but he was there, all the same.

Every garden had a root of Elecampane, or Helenium, the root of which was used as a medicine for some common diseases. There was also a bunch of Lavender, one of Rue, one of Garlic, a bed of Thyme, one of Chamomile: a bunch of Balm, some Parsley and some Sage, a bed of Tansey, and some Wormwood.

Of the plants in her herb bed, John's grandmother would have found the garlic, parsley, thyme, and sage of use in cooking, and the lavender good for scenting her laundry, but John lumps the eleven together because they formed the major weapons against illness in her pharmacopoeia. It is well to remember that the family did not have so much as aspirin, and as John makes clear later on, even physicians grasped at herbal straws.

The herbs John mentions had for thousands of years helped man against a wide range of his ailments. In the *Proceedings* of the Columbus Horticultural Society, Vol. 1, 1886, pp. 111-114, John enlarged upon the healing properties of the plants, but with typical Victorian reticence did not mention that six of the eleven were used in treating "female complaints." Possibly he did not know of such uses, but his grandmother and his aunts certainly did. Elecampane, lavender, rue, thyme, camomile, and tansy have a history of use by women in their "difficult times."

In the article on his grandmother's garden for the Columbus Horticultural Society, John mentioned her fruit trees, her vegetables, and her flowers, but paid especial attention to her herbs. Elecampane, for instance, was a tonic and stimulant used in "pectoral syrups" and in the treatment of hydrophobia. Lavender, besides scenting linen, "was cultivated for its cordial and stomachic properties." Rue was a base for bitters. Garlic was esteemed as a vermifuge. John mentions only the fragrance of thyme, but it was the source for thymol, which even today has a list of uses. In his article John mentioned the value of thymol, but connected it with sweet marjoram, which his grandmother also grew. He wrote: "I have found a very light application of the oil a prompt remedy for fungus or mouldiness on book bindings." The camomile John remembered as "an aromatic bitters, deservedly popular as a tonic." It had indeed long been known to soothe the nerves: Peter Rabbit's mother gave him camomile tea after a hard day. Balm was good for fevers, and John remarked, "Balm tea I well remember." Parsley had other uses than as a flavoring—"the root a popular diuretic."

Elsewhere in this autobiography John insists on plenty of sage in his sausage. For the Columbus Horticultural Society he quoted an unnamed source that called it "a good gargle." John added, "We sometimes drank it at table instead of tea." He quoted, concerning tansy, "Bitter and aromatic, and the infusion is a very popular domestic medicine." John added, "During the summer we were rarely without a bottle of tansy bitters in the house." Not recognizing wormwood's fame as a narcotic, John noted only its qualities as a tonic and vermifuge.

After adding saffron to the list given in his autobiography, he nostalgically wrote: "To the rafters in the attic—no, we had no attic—in the garret or the kitchen loft, would be found a supply of these things, together with thorough-wort or boneset, which could always be relied upon as an emetic; it could be used as a tonic or cathartic, acording to the dose. Hoarhound...was used as a tea for coughs. Some pennyroyal....'Warmly aromatic, and the infusion is a deservedly popular diaphoretic, carminative, etc.'...There would be some mustard...in a bag or package....We could not buy it prepared, but pulverized it with the rolling pin on the dough-trough lid, and used it at the table or as a plaster to allay pain.

"With these the grandmother was prepared to administer to nearly all the ailments of the family, and about all the calls the doctor made were to bleed the dear old woman at not infrequent intervals."

Much can be learned about the true medicinal value of herbs from the works listed in the bibliography. Henrietta A. Diers Rau is willing to enlarge upon the virtues of herbs and thus gives, perhaps, a better picture of what they meant to our forebears. Anyone with access to the 11th edition of the *Encyclopedia Britannica* will find there much encapsulated information that does not appear in the later editions.

On one side of the garden were two flower beds, about ten feet square each. In the corner of one was a bunch of white lilies which grew every year without any care, in a cluster of a dozen or more stalks, and a bunch of beautiful white lilies on every stalk, with a perfume not excelled by any.

In the beds were pinks, single only, and colored from pure white to bright red. They also were hardy and had a fragrance not excelled by any grown now. There were annual flowers in abundance, Marigolds, bachelor's button, cockscomb, and others which have not only gone out of memory but out of cultivation. The nasturtium was cultivated not so much for its blossoms as for its seed capsules which made a very spicy pickle.

There was a bed of Asparagus (Sparrergrass) but while it always grew freely, no use was made of it but to put in the parlor fireplace after the fires were discontinued or to hang up for the flies to roost on. The idea of eating it we never heard of.

There were always hollyhocks growing and being self-sown, were all single. There were a large number of roses, but they were all of the old "hundred leaved" compact rose [*i.e.* the cabbage rose, *Rosa centifolia*]. There was an Althea tree [rose of Sharon], for it was a tree, not a bush, and a root of Chrysathemum that was hardy, and always bloomed freely, and so late that the bloom was almost always covered with snow.

SCHOOL

I commenced going to school when I was in my sixth year, and I walked two miles to school. I had listened to so many Indian and Ghost stories told by farm hands and men in my uncles shoe shop that I had become very fearful of ghosts and other fancies, and was very timid. About half the way to school, the road was through a thick woods, and if I had no companion, as was sometimes the case, as soon as I entered the woods, I would start on a run, and would run all the way through it.

A mere remnant of this woods, several times logged, still exists on the road between Purcellville and Lincoln. The editor's father remembered a time, when he was a boy in the 1870's, that the woods grew solid for much of the way between the two towns and had not yet been logged for the first time.

The little brick schoolhouse of one room that lay at the end of John's two-mile trip was new then, having been built in 1815. It still stands near the Goose Creek Friends' Meeting House in Lincoln, and is included on the autumn Dirt Roads Tour.

The school house was of brick, though there were school houses, log ones, in every neighborhood. When I first went to school, there was a

John's school is still sometimes open.

long row of double desks, reaching entirely across one side of the house. They were made of heavy, wide yellow pine boards, and had hinged lids. If a lid happened to slip from our fingers, it would come down with a bang that would startle the whole school. On the other side of the house was an old desk brought from the old log school house, which was simply a double writing desk with a bench along each side for the pupils, with a box underneath into which we could put our books and slates, and on the tops and edges all sorts of work of the boys knives. The seats were long benches reaching the entire length of the desk, so that every boy and girl, except the one at each end, had to climb over the bench, to get into his or her seat. A few years after I commenced going to school this desk was superceded by good, well-made and convenient desks.

Every pupil had to furnish his or her own books, paper, slate, quills and ink. The teacher made the pens and mended them. I learned to make a good pen, and many of the children seemed to think I made a better pen than the teacher, and he was glad to be relieved.

The system of teaching writing was wholly different from the present, but I think was equally as efficient. Ruled paper, as well as steel pens were not yet in use. We had to rule our own copy books, and had to make them first. The only paper we could buy was "fools cap" [paper 13 by 16 or 17 inches]. Every pupil had a lead pencil for ruling the copy made out of a piece of lead, hammered into the proper shape, which answered the purpose perfectly. My uncle brought me the first "black lead pencil" ever seen in the school, which cost twenty five cents. It was about three inches long, a little larger than the lead pencil of today and covered with paper, with no wood.

An insert tipped into the earliest version reads: "Paper machines were invented in 1803 or 1804, but the paper we used in school was made in single sheets one sheet at a time. The pulp from which the paper was made was ground and mixed with water, and a wire screen like a modern window screen, made of fine wire, and of the proper size for the sheet wanted was used. They would have sheets of fine felt of the same size, one of which sheets would be spread on a suitable stand, when the screen would be dipped into the pulp, and the water draining off, the frame was turned over on the felt leaving the sheet of paper sticking to it. When a sufficient number of sheets were made, they were put into a press and the water pressed out. The sheets were then hung upon strings to dry. This left the sheet rough, or as the book-sellers now say, "deckel-edged," from the frame in which the sheets are moulded which is called a deckle.

"Now a machine will turn out a sheet of any length or any desired width, and cut it in any required sheets. A short time after I came to Columbus, there was a paper mill built here with a modern machine. One of the editors of the city in a description called it a "four-drainer" machine. On meeting him, I complimented him on his discription but said "you made a bad balk in the name of the machine. It is not "four-drainer" but Fourdrinier, after the name of the Frenchman who invented it." "Is that so? Well, now see here. Don't you tell any body else that, for you are the only man in Columbus who knows it."

The pupil was first taught to make straight lines by such a copy as this   ///

and when he could do that, then
between two wider lines thus

The next lesson was the loops

This was doubled in length,
and then inverted:

These exercises were continued until the child had acquired a good use of the pen, and then a "large hand" copy was given, which was a copy to fill the space between two lines. This was followed by a "small hand" or business hand. There was a good supply of copies on the teacher's desk neatly engrossed and pasted on card board; "paste board" really, for we had not heard of card board. This system would now be thought not only out of date, but probably absurd, but it produced as good results as any subsequent method.

Our school generally numbered in the winter about seventy: not quite so many in the summer. We had but one teacher, but after I became old enough, he would ask me to hear a spelling or reading class when he found a busy day. We never heard of a woman teacher. One special qualification for a teacher was the ability to whip any boy in school, and a week rarely passed without the switch being used. There was one boy who seemed to think the week a failure unless he got a switching.

> A century later only a few teachers at Lincoln were still using corporal punishment, and those applied it only to the shrinking palm of the outstretched hand.

The teacher always kept one and usually two switches or "rods" above the window. The kind preferred was a gum or hickory sprout about as large at the butt end as a mans little finger, and about three feet long.

They were supple and elastic and would bend to fit a boy exactly. One of our teachers dressed out a rod from white oak which soon got stiff and hard and was really barbarous.

The pupils were not punished after school and privately, but before the whole school, some of the boys laughing and some of the girls crying. I never was punished but once. Three of us were sitting on a bench by the stove; the two on each side of me kept whispering across my face. I asked them to quit, and with my head down and on my book, I was startled by the switch across our backs. I told the teacher the facts, but he had not the manhood to apologize to me, which I confess in this late day of my life, I have never been able to entirely excuse him.

There was but slight attempt at classification in the school. There were two classes in spelling, one from the spelling book, of which we had two kinds, Comly's and Webster's; and one class in the Dictionary. We stood in a line, and a word missed passed down the line until it was spelled correctly, when the one spelling it went above the one who first missed it. I well remember the first time I spelled in class. It consisted of about fifteen boys and girls, for we had co-education. A word was given out at about the middle of the class. I knew at once how to spell it, and it came down to me. I spelled it correctly, and marched half way up, the proudest boy in school.

Our place in class was kept on a list of slips of pasteboard attached to a strip of the same with slits in it, by which the names could be correctly arranged. When the class was called up, the names were called out from that register. When it was dismissed the teacher called out No. 1, and the pupil at the head gave the name and so on down the line, the teacher correcting the list. I almost always stood near the head.

We had four reading classes. One in the spelling book, which had reading lessons, [and] one each in Murray's Introduction to the English Reader, the English Reader and the Sequel to the English Reader. We were not taught reading very wisely. The head of the class read a sentence and every one of the class followed with a sentence, but little attention being paid by any pupil to any thing but the "stops" [that is, the punctuation marks]. Many years after, when I came to teach reading, I would have one pupil read a sentence, then have the next one read the same sentence, correcting any [errors] in pronunciation, pauses, emphasis, or any thing else, and so on till some one read it correctly.

We had no classes in Arithmetic. Every pupil had an arithmetic and a slate and pencil. Our Arithmetic began with pages of sums without the answers. I well remember the first day I had a slate, I filled both sides with questions in addition, handed my slate to the teacher, who marked them all correct, and I went home that night bragging.

On Friday afternoon we "said the tables," beginning with the multiplication tables and reciting a long list, including Federal Money, English Money, Apothecaries Weight, Avoirdupois Weight, Troy Weight, Decimals, Long Measure, Square Measure, Land Measure and some others I can't recall.

Geography had not been taught until I was about twelve years old. We studied Woodbridge and Willards Geography.

When I was about fourteen years old, I was handed a copy of Comly's Grammar, in which a class was to be formed. The first thing we were asked to do was to commit to memory page after page of definitions and rules and exceptions to rules, for which I could not see any possible use. I disliked memorizing, and declined to join the class, but soon after, a travelling lecturer on grammar came into the neighborhood who offered to let me into a class with the agreement that I might attend a week, and if I was not satisfied I might quit. I became interested the first day, attended two classes [two courses of classes?], and got a fair acquaintance with grammar. He required no memorizing except the parts of speech until you saw the use for what you committed. Of all the tasks ever assigned, memorizing was the most irksome. I never committed but one piece of poetry by rote, and no prose.

I went through Pike's Arithmetic, and then studied Harney's Mensuration, which includes measurements of all kinds, surfaces, solids, and liquids. I then studied Gummere's Surveying, which proved of use to me afterwards in land surveying, and then Algebra. I was the only pupil that studied these branches and they were the highest taught in the school. In [Algebra] my teacher could not take me through the book. He had been a pupil at Fair Hill Boarding School, the leading school of the Society of Friends at that time, but his teacher could go no further than to Cubic Equations. Afterward when I began teaching, three boys asked me if I could teach Algebra. I said yes, and I took them through the book (Bonnycastle) with a good deal of feeling bordering on contempt for a teacher who had been to a boarding school who could say he could not do it.

Fair Hill Boarding School, under the care of the Baltimore Yearly Meeting of Friends, stood in what is now Olney, Maryland. The fine old building burnt down only a year or so ago. Fair Hill, which in 1823 reported an attendance of 42, was in constant financial trouble because of its low charges, and so Friends were continually passing the hat for it.

John's own education was heavily weighted in favor of Friendly principles. Three of the authors of his textbooks were Quakers: John Gummere's *Treatise on Surveying* ran through 22 editions; John Comly's grammar and spelling book were adopted in many schools of the Midwest, Southern, and Western states; Lindley Murray's various readers had a phenomenal success from their first appearance in 1799 and appeared again and again for decades. Comly's speller set its tone early, with the first of its reading selections: "All of us, my son, are to die."

Non-Quaker William C. Woodbridge's *Universal Geography*, with a section on ancient geography by the famous educator Emma Willard, appeared in 1824, when John was 12, just as he says.

Our school was under the care of the Goose Creek Monthly Meeting of Friends, and once a month a committee of three men would come on Friday afternoon to examine the school. We had to read and spell before the committee, and to prepare a specimen of our writing, of two lines "coarse" and two lines "fine" hand and that was the examination. The committee was composed of honest, but generally illiterate men. Our school house was about one hundred yards from the meeting house, and the pupils (and many of them were not members) were all required to attend meeting every Fifth Day (Thursday), which many felt to be rather a bore.

We marched back and forth in double file, and I never knew but one case of breaking the column. The moment we were out of the meeting house one of the most decorous boys in the school broke ranks and ran to the school house at the top of his speed. As I entered the house he shouted to me, "I've got it John, I've got it," thus following Archimedes who is recorded as running naked through the streets shouting "Eureka! Eureka" when he had found the means of detecting a dishonest goldsmiths fraud.

Hook had become well known in the neighborhood for his ability in solving knotty questions in arithmetic: and any person in the neighborhood in possession of such a question sent it to him. We had no pencils to carry in our pockets: but many of us carried a piece of chalk and Hook kept the barn and crib doors covered with figures by his attempts to solve a specially knotty question. While sitting in meeting, the solution of one became plain to him: and he was so excited he broke ranks and the rule as soon as he passed the door.

> Showing that one can do better when assisted by higher authority. Lincoln Friends have a saying that the best barns in the area were built during Meeting for Worship.

We had for our government a set of rules which covered four pages of fools cap which were read to us every Friday afternoon. They descended into minute details, such as that we must not enter any inclosure on our way to or from school, and this with the knowledge that a large per cent of us crossed fields going and coming because the distance was shorter. It was not at all an uncommon thing for one boy to snatch another boy's hat off his head and throw it over a fence, in order to make him violate the rule by climbing the fence to get it.

Friends who had colored boys living with them sent them to school along with their own children. There were two mulatto and one negro boy who attended our school, and they were taught and treated just as the other children were by both teacher and pupils. After I had lived in Ohio several years, I took my wife and little son to Cincinnati, and put them on a steam boat on their way to Virginia. A mulatto man on the boat came to me, and I found him to be my school mate of 25 years before:[33] Bill Coleman, and he was steward of the boat.

I attended school one winter in a pioneer school house, because I felt sure I could beat the man Friends had employed as a teacher [*i. e.* find a better teacher]. It was built as all pioneer school houses were, of round unhewn logs, chinked and daubed, that is the spaces between the logs were filled with wood or stones, which were plastered over. [There was] a door in the center of the south side with a four pane "7x9" window along side it, another similar window in the west end and another on the north side made by cutting out a log so as to leave space for a window of say half a dozen panes of 7 x 9 glass. We used no larger panes. A large desk for the teacher stood at the window near the door. The fireplace occupied the east side of the house and would take in a four foot stick of wood and a six plate stove in the center of the room. On one side of the house, a board about two feet wide was fastened, slanting, for a writing desk, with a box under it in which books and slates could be kept. On the other side of the room there was a double one of the same sort so that pupils could sit on either side. The seats were made of slabs smooth side up, with legs fixed in holes bored in the slabs. There was a floor overhead of unmatched boards laid loose. The roof was not shingled but covered with clapboards split from oak timber, not shaved, and held in place on the roof by heavy poles reaching the whole length of the building, and held in place by poles at the ends, hence called a "stake and rider" roof.

Nearly all the school houses in that section were of that kind. I knew of but two brick ones and they were both built by Quakers.

Barring the teacher out on Christmas day was a favorite amusement in many of the schools. As I sat at my desk (I took one from home) I noticed the boys all collecting in the school room. They said, "We are going to bar the master out," and they proceeded to fasten the door. They soon became so noisy that I asked them to let me out. On coming from home, where he had gone for his dinner, the "master" (we had no school "teachers," they were, very properly school "masters") seeing no boys out at play, knew what it meant and went home. Some teachers treated the boys with ginger cakes or apples.

A few years before the end of the century, the teacher at the Goose Creek school that John had attended was still being barred out on Christmas Day. (Word of mouth from one of his students.)

Loudoun historian Eugene M. Scheel believes that the "pioneer schoolhouse" attended by John for one winter was probably the one built about the time of the Revolution near what is now the center of Purcellville, Va., by James and Rebekah Dillon. They were Friends and wished to educate their own five children and those of neighbors. See Scheel's *The Story of Purcellville, Loudoun County, Virginia.* Purcellville, 1978, pp. 3-4.

Christmas was treated just as any other day except by the negros and the rougher portion of the population. It was common with the childre~ to try to cry "christmas gift" first to every one of the family ~ ˙

met on Christmas morning, but very rarely did any gift follow, and when it did, it was some trifle of no value. There was no systematic giving as at present. I have no recollection of ever receiving any thing of any value except a very little book my teacher gave me: and my school mates and playmates never had any that I knew of.[34]

The teachers of that [day] had not learned that "Love is the greatest thing in the world" and many of them do not yet.

None of our "Schoolmasters" equaled some of those of New England in cruel ingenuity. Some "schoolmasters whipped on the soles of the feet." "One instructor made his scholars sit on a bark seat turned upside down with his thumb in the knot of a floor." "Another master of the inquisition invented a unipod—a stool with one leg—sometimes placed in the middle of the seat, sometimes on the edge, on which the unfortunate scholar tiresomely balanced. Others sent out the suffering pupil to cut a branch of a tree, and, making a split in the large end, sprung it on the culprit's nose." (Miss Earle)[35]

None of our schoolmasters equalled these in ingenuity, but some of them did have a "dunce block," a stool or block of wood, placed in the middle of the floor, on which the pupil was made to sit.

Some of the colonial teachers were transported felons, and in Pennsylvania they were "redemptioners," who had the ability to write well and some knowledge of arithmetic: but the teachers of Friends schools were nearly always members of the society and fairly educated in the main branches.

Two weeks at harvest time was the only vacation our school had, and then the boys and girls were needed to carry sheaves for shocking and to help around the house.

Of childrens books we had none. I never saw a Mother Goose, nor any thing of the kind in the neighborhood.

There were some pictures in some of our school books which are, now, amusing. In Comly's Spelling book, which was compiled by John Comly, an eminent minister of the Society of Friends, it had in it reading lessons, some of them illustrated. One is about the wren, and a picture of the bird is more than half the height of the house before which it stands.

Another lesson about the whale had a picture of the whale, which is spouting out two columns of water, nearly half as high as the masts of the ship close by. They had not learned that the whale was merely breathing, and that it did not breathe water, but only a little spray.

In our geographies, we had a picture illustrating the Maelstrom. A ship was shown under full sail, going round in a circle with a deep center, in which it was doomed to be drawn, and the history verifying the picture.

Another picture showed a ship trying hard to escape Scylla on one side & Charybdis on the other, with reading to match. Both these dangers of the ocean vanished.

But these were not so bad as those in our illustrated Bibles. In the first one I owned, a pocket one, bound in Morocco, gilt edged and fully illustrated, among the pictures was one in which a whale is pitching Jonah head foremost on the dry ground. Another represents Samson with his knee on a lions back, and holding it to the ground, while with a hand in each jaw he was pulling his jaws off. A third had a bear killing the children, "forty and two" of them, and Elisha looking on. A fourth showed Josephs brothers throwing him into the pit.

From these and like pictures we learned many things which we had to unlearn afterwards.[36]

CHILDREN'S CLOTHING

Children were dressed plainly, but not sufficiently. I wore in the winter Kentucky jeans pantaloons, which was cotton chain and wool filling, twilled in weaving, which throws the wool on top. I wore no drawers nor underclothing of any kind: woolen stockings up to the knee, low shoes just up to the lower edge of the ankle bone. I wore, over my shirt, a wrapper or "wamus" [warm jacket] of cotton and wool, with sleeves, and reaching down to my waist over that, a woolen jacket and a "roundabout" [short jacket]. I never wore any thing around my neck but the shirt collar until I was fourteen years old.

I was dressed as warmly as any other boy in the school. In going home from school I frequently had to face the north-west wind, and I have a very distinct recollection that I have many times felt a smarting sensation on the front of my thighs as though the skin was cracking.

I never passed a winter without "bad colds" and sore throat, so that I could not recite my lessons, but I always went to school. My grandmother used to apply several remedies. One for sore throat was "Goose grease." When a goose was roasted, the grease that came from it was saved for such purposes and I felt sure it relieved my throat. If the doctors are correct in their opinion that many of such diseases are microbic, this was a scientific prescription, for oil of any kind applied to an organism of that kind will kill it.

> We can easily understand John's fuzziness about the germ theory of disease. After all, he was in his late fifties and early sixties when it was coming into general acceptance.

They made several different remedies: hoarhound tea, and ginger tea among them. Another was a "stew" made of whiskey, butter and ginger.

I was dressed as well as any boy in school and fared as well as any.

The girls nearly all dressed in calico. Some wore "linsey," cotton and wool.

> John is being absent minded. Linsey was *linen* and wool—hence the full name, "linsey-woolsey."

They all wore woolen petticoats but no drawers of any kind, and their arms and chests were very poorly or entirely unprotected. A woman or girl could not have been induced to wear drawers. It would have been thought indecent. They were for men's wear.

So far was this sentiment carried that if a young man happened to come upon a girl at work upon any of her underclothing, especially a "Shift" ("chemise," "shimmy" came in use later) he would at once inquire what she was making, which she would always evade. The story was told of a neighboring girl who was found by a young man actually at work upon a "shift," of which he accused her. To prove that he was mistaken, she actually spoiled her garment by turning it into a pillow case.[37]

I never had any kind of an overcoat until I was seventeen years old. I then had one made of wool sheared from our own sheep sent to the carding machine, carded into rolls, spun at home, and taken to the factory where it was woven and died a plain drab, and taken to the neighboring tailor, who made a coat. Overcoats all had capes, some a single cape, extending half way down to the elbows, [or], as mine was, with a narrow cape, three or four inches wide, with narrow strips, about two inches wide sewed on so as to look like a double cape. Mine had four such imitations, this making it have the appearance of a four fold cape.

There was rarely any time during the winter at which there were not boys and girls in school unable to recite their lessons, on account of "bad colds." Neither boys nor girls were dressed at all as they should be, and many of them suffered all their lives as a result. I have gone through my whole life suffering from nasal catarrh, the result of insufficient clothing in my childhood.

WINTER

There were almost every winter, heavy snow storms. They were nearly always badly drifted: for a snow storm nearly always was followed by a north-west gale, which blew with such force that scarcely a winter passed without fences being blown down, sometimes twenty to forty rods at a stretch.

> Available evidence shows that winters during the 1820's were indeed severe. The "Little Ice Age" that had gripped the world for generations did not end till the mid-1800's. But in 1900, when John recalled his blizzard, the present genial period—perhaps the warmest in thousands of years—was well under way. For more, see the article on climate by Samuel W. Matthews in the *National Geographic* for November 1976.

One of the worst snow storms I ever knew commenced on Friday, while we were at play at noon. When school was dismissed, it was three inches deep, and by Saturday night, it was just two feet. Then the "norwest" wind came on and by Sunday night the roads were blocked: many of them as to be impassable, and remained so about six weeks. Sleds and sleighs went where they pleased, over fences (the tops of the stakes only being visible) and across fields.

I did not try to go to school on Monday morning, but on Tuesday I concluded to ride. I rode a "spunky" little horse, and before I got out of sight of the house, I entered a lane drifted full of snow for about a quarter of a mile, nearly to the top of the fence. Where the snow was piled up, there was a narrow pass along the leeward side, through which I thought I could push Charley, but he did not like it. When we had got about half way past the drift, with a sudden leap he landed right in the middle of it, with nothing but his head visible and my legs spread out on top of the snow. With another leap the girth broke and he left me sitting in the saddle. He made a leap or two and then turned and plunged through the drift, going entirely under, except his head. I sat and watched him until he got nearly home, when I shouldered the saddle and started back. I struck across the fields, and soon came to a low place about one hundred and fifty yards across, in which the snow came up to my arms, but it had not yet become hard, and I pulled, or pushed, through.

By the next morning the snow had become so compacted by the wind that I found I could walk on the surface, and I did so for six weeks. The air turned warmer one night, and the snow began to soften. When school was dismissed next day, I found I could not walk on its top, and took the road. The snow had been packed down in the road by sleds and sleighs, until it was more than "half knee deep"; and it had melted until it was full of water and so soft that at every few steps my foot would go to the ground. I never knew when I sat my foot down whether it would stay on top or go through a foot below. It need not be said that was a tiresome walk.

While the snow was lying, I took a memorable ride. Dr Albert Heaton, a near neighbor was dying of consumption. Like all such cases, he had tried and was willing to try any remedy which offered any hope, and he wished to try Dr Carpenters Compound Syrup of Liverwort, which was largely advertised as a remedy for diseases of the lungs. He had failed to get it, and sent to know if I would go to Washington for him, to which I assented. There was no railroad nor no stage, and the only way was on horse back. The people had not learned to "break" the roads, at such times as they do in New England, so that I found the road for the whole distance, forty five miles, without a vehicle track, except two or three miles on each side of Leesburg. I rode the distance between breakfast and supper, and rode it again the next day, in the teeth of a nor-west wind punctuated, at frequent intervals, by a brisk snow squall. The doctor's over shoes, great coat and gloves kept me warm, but the medicine did him no good.

GAMES

Our games at school were very much like those now played, but they have been much modified. We played town ball, from which base ball has grown. We used a softer and lighter ball, and struck it with our hands instead of a club, but our bases were the same. The rules were not so complicated.

We also played foot ball but the brutality of the present game (1900) was not yet invented.

John's date. It was perhaps a form of his game, by then called "soccer," that Lincoln schoolchildren were still playing a century later.

With the small ones, marbles was a favorite. We played a game which I think is the foundation of golf. We called it "nucks." We would make three holes, about four or five feet apart, in a line. Then, with three players, the game was to get your marble into all three of the holes three times, going down, up, and down again. The one who did that first was the winner, and the one who was last had to take his marble between the knuckles of his fore and middle finger, hold his hand in the second hole, and let the other two shoot at the marble three times apiece, from the first hole, hitting the marble or the knuckles as their accuracy in shooting or their honesty might determine. From this part of the game came the term "knucks" or "knuckles." Every player had the right to keep the others away from the holes by knocking them away with his own marble if he could. I was an acknowledged expert at marbles, as I was at nearly all the games. I was active, and liked to play.

One of the amusements was pitching "quates" (quoits) or the old large copper cents or sometimes half dollars or dollars if they were to be had. We did not have the neat iron quoits afterwards used but selected suitable stones from the field or brook. We would drive two pegs (megs) in the ground, say twenty feet apart. Sides were chosen, every one pitching two cents, or two "quates" and the one who got nearest the "meg" was the winner. When the "quate" or cent was pitched so as to lean against the meg, that counted two.

Friends were not only opposed to, but prohibited all games of chance and we had no such games in our school, but one day my cousin Lewis and I went to a mill dam three miles off and there found some boys pitching cents. They were accustomed to pitching "for keeps"; that is the winner of the game took all the cents around the meg: so that if there were four pitchers, he would get eight cents, including his own. They soon challenged us to pitch a game. We knew we could beat them, and accepted the challenge. In about twenty minutes we had all their cents in our pockets. Pitching cents and playing marbles "for keeps" were not allowed in our school. While they were both an exercise of skill, there was just enough of "getting something for nothing" in them to cause Friends to prohibit them.

A favorite game was "corner ball," which was played by any number, not less than four on a side. To play it, first make a "bull pen," which was usually about twenty or thirty feet square with trees or stumps for corners if they could be properly located; if not, stones. Sides were chosen, not limited in number. Two boys would be agreed upon to choose sides. One of them would take a stick about a foot long, toss it into the air, when the other would catch it. The first would take hold of it just above the hand of the one holding it, and so on until one of them held it by the upper end. So on, three times, and the one who had it at the top twice had first choice. They would then choose alternately until all who wished to play were chosen. This was "tossing up" and "choosing sides."

To play the game four boys would take their places at the corners, and four on the other side would go in the "bull pen." The ball must be thrown round the pen twice and across diagonally twice without touching the ground; if any boy missed it, it must be started again. When it was properly tossed round, it was "hot." Then the one holding it could throw at one inside, and if he was hit, those inside could in return hit one at the corners, who always ran away to avoid it. If one was hit, he was out and his place taken by another: if not the one throwing was out, and so on till one side was all out. If a ball thrown at you was caught by one of your side before it touched the ground or at the first bounce, the thrower was out. The ball used was, so far as I knew, always made of yarn ravelled out of old stockings, wound tightly and covered with calf-skin.

This was one of our most popular and interesting games with the larger boys. It gave us good exercise, and required quickness, alertness and skill in throwing, catching and dodging. A boy was rarely injured. I was once knocked down by a ball striking me on the jaw, and at another time my eye was "bunged up."

"Trap" was played by making a hole in the ground big enough to hold the ball. Take a piece of shingle or thin board for a "treadle," stick one end of it in the hole, place the ball on it; trip the ball in the air with a "paddle," strike it and send it flying. If the other side catch it, either before or at the first bounce, the striker was out. When all at the bat were caught out, the other side took the bat.

The younger boys played "Antony Over." We played it over a large, vacant stone Meeting House. We chose sides and took stations on opposite sides of the house. When ready the signal "Antony" was given, and if the other side was ready, the answer came, "Over," when the ball was thrown over the house. If caught, the catcher ran to the other side of the house and hit one of the other side if he could, and took him back to his side. The object was to get all the boys on one side, and then that side had the game. These ball games all gave us good exercise.

A hundred years later the same game, by then called "Annie Over," was still being played, but over the one-room building where John had gone to school. The old vacant Meeting House had become a residence, owned by the Meeting. It is still used as a home.

We had several games which were played by running only. "Prisoners Base" was popular. Two boys would be selected as leaders. They would toss up for choice of players, and choose sides. Two bases were chosen, with us always trees, about one hundred yards apart, with two "Prisoner's bases," about thirty or forty feet from the bases, at a right angle with the line joining them. The game was for a boy to start from his base, when one from the other base would start after him. If he caught him, which meant merely to touch him, he took him to their prisoners base: and if one side could get all the other side prisoners, it had the game.

Sometimes there would be half a dozen from each side out [running] at once, and we must always know who left his base last, because one who left his base after I did could catch me, but I could not catch him. If you could manage to recapture a prisoner he went home, and into the game again. Care must be taken to have a boy at the base all the time, for if one of the other side touched your base without being touched, that counted a game.

"Old Man" or "Fox and Hounds" was also a favorite. Sides were not chosen in this game. A base was chosen, always a tree. A boy would start out and go into the woods. We had at our school about two hundred acres of thick forest for a play ground. After he had gone about two hundred yards, or far enough to be out of sight, he would give a shout, when all the rest would start out in the chase to catch him, while his aim would be to get back to the base without being caught.

These games were exciting and furnished a complete substitute for a gymnasium: for an hours exercise such as they gave was enough for one day.

Some of the "little boys" had for amusement pop-guns, some made of the barrel of a large goose quill with a slice of raw potato for wadding, or an elder squirt, bows and arrows, willow whistles, kites, and occasionally you could see a corn-stalk fiddle. Take a piece of corn stalk, between two joints loosen the hard outside fiber about half an inch wide, put a bit of stick under each end to raise it from the stalk. Prepare another in the same way for a bow, and you have a corn stalk fiddle.

> A present-day John Janney, second cousin thrice removed of his namesake, tells the editors that Lincoln children still play Prisoner's Base, just as we also did between the two Johns. Fox and Hounds (known to us as Fox and Geese, and called that by John in his 1907 text) was still being played in the 1920's, but no longer. The thick forest necessary for the game has shriveled to some three acres, still owned by the Meeting but only sparsely wooded and split by roads and a field. Every now and then another of the great old oaks topples. Incidentally, if you ever make a cornstalk fiddle, remember to rub rosin on the "strings."

Kites were very popular. The larger boys would make them large enough to carry an oiled paper lantern at the end of the tail which on a dark night were likely to attract the attention of the neighbors. Sometimes they would make a rocket out of elders and so place it in the lantern as to be fired off when the candle burned low enough, when the rocket would come blazing to the ground.

In bad weather the small boys had the use of an old log meeting house[38] which stood just across the road from the school house. It had no floor, and furnished plenty of room for marbles or Poor Pussy Wants a Corner, which was a favorite with small boys and girls. The game was, and is, for it is still played: for four boys or girls to take a corner, and then to change corners without letting some one get your corner from you. To make it complete, one or more of those without corners must be calling out, "Poor Pussie Wants a Corner."

Jumping the rope was the favorite amusement for the girls. They did not have the ropes with handles now used, but got neat little grape vines from the woods or fence rows. There were two kinds; one long rope turned by a girl (or a boy) at each end, in which three or four girls could jump at once: the other a single one, and the contest was to see who could jump the oftenest without tripping. It was not rare for a little girl to jump fifty times, and sometimes one hundred without tripping or missing.

Jumping the rope where two were turning was a good exercise. A girl would jump the rope and run around the one turning, and jump the rope the other way, and then around the girl at that end. Half a dozen of them could jump together.

Tossing "Jack-stones" was another favorite amusement with girls. They did not have the neat little cast ones they can now have, but used the prettiest little gravel they could find.

WORK: MILK AND EGGS

Every farm in that section was well supplied with never-failing springs of good soft water, but nearly all the houses were built away from the spring on higher ground, and so the women carried all the water needed for all household purposes rarely less than a hundred yards and in many cases twice and in some cases three times that distance. We had a good stone milk house, and our folks built a stone fire place near it, near the spring, at which they did their washing and cheese making in fair and warm weather.

There was a stone spring house, or "milk house" on every farm. Every farmer's wife made cheese, but the cheese they made would not sell today.

My grandmother made excellent butter, and milking about half a dozen cows she sold a good deal. A huckster called once in two weeks to get her butter, eggs, and such other things as she might have to sell. One huckster who came regularly during several years was a Scotch-Irishman, who usually managed to get to our house so as to stay all night, which the younger ones were glad of, for we enjoyed his Irish stories. One I specially remember. He was an earnest Catholic, and heartily believed in the Orthodox Devil. He said, One day when his father was at church and while the Priest was preaching, the Devil walked into the church and walked up towards the pulpit. The Priest dropped on his knees and commenced praying to the Lord to drive him away. The Devil only laughed at that, whereupon the Priest caught up the Bible and flung it at the Devil, who was so scared that he did not take time to go out at the door, but flew out and took the whole end of the church with him. I cannot tell the story as he told it. He seemed to believe it as surely as he believed any thing else.

Our women did one thing I have not known done since. A day or two before the huckster was expected, they would put some clean water in a tub, mix a little vinegar with it, and put all the eggs in it. Those that were spoiled would float, and were thrown away. The rest were washed as clean as when first laid, so that when their eggs went to market, they were tempting and could be warranted fresh. You will look in vain for such eggs in the markets of this city [Columbus].

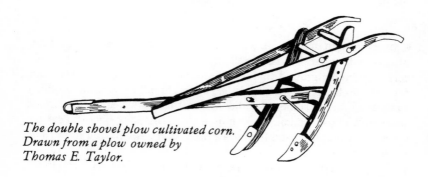

The double shovel plow cultivated corn.
Drawn from a plow owned by
Thomas E. Taylor.

WORK: THE FARM YEAR

I knew but two renters in the neighborhood, outside the little cross-roads village. The farms were worked by the owner and his sons with the aid of a "bound" boy, and a hired man or more if needed in the summer.[39]

Our summer work commenced in the spring, to fix the fences. We would go over them all, supply broken rails and re-set stakes. The fences were nearly all "worm" fences, and the best ones were "nine rails and double rider," making a fence eight to nine feet high. A single rider fence left a space between the "rider" or top rail and the one next below it through which a cow or horse could put its head and lift the rider off and then jump the fence, but the double rider closed that opening.

> Worm fences are also called snake fences—in other words, they are ordinary zig-zag rail fences. Barbed wire would not be marketed for another half century, and wire mesh would not be available till after that.

As soon as the ground was fit, we plowed for corn. The old rule was to plant corn as soon as the hickory leaves got to be as big as a squirrel's ears, and planting and cultivation kept us busy until mowing time. We had never heard of a mowing machine, but did all the mowing with the scythe. When I was old enough to use a scythe, I was given the worst one on the farm as was usual, and it was very hard work for me.

When we needed a scythe snead, we could not buy one from the store as can be done now, but must go into the woods and find a limb of the proper shape, trim it to size, and go to the blacksmith to get the proper irons made. Our scythes were made in New England and were of two kinds: the Waldron, a short broad scythe and the Black-snake, a long narrow one. Our meadows were merely natural grass, "June grass."

> Waldron was a make of scythe, not a shape; A.M.J. still has a Waldron scythe. The two kinds of scythes, as John describes them, seem to correspond to what we grew up calling the bush scythe and the grass scythe. A scythe snead is a scythe handle. A.M.J. uses the term today, even if it is an older form more modern "snathe" or "snath."

Many farmers stacked their hay, but we had a large barn, the mows of which held all the hay we mowed, and we therefore never stacked any.

We had never heard of corn planters, row droppers, they were not yet invented. After the ground was plowed and harrowed, the common practice was to mark it out with a shovel plow, running furrows across each way about three feet apart, thus dividing the field into squares about three feet on a side. Instead of this, the best farmers marked out the field with a mould board plow which threw up a ridge on one side, and by running the plow back and throwing the earth up against the ridge already made, a ridge of loose earth was thrown up. The field was thus divided into parallel ridges about three feet apart, with a "balk" [an unplowed strip] between them about a foot wide. Furrows were run across these ridges: three feet apart and corn dropped at the intersections with the ridges. The advantage of this method was that when the corn was harrowed, when it was about four or five inches high, the ridges were leveled down, and the ground left mellow.

The favorite spot for the nest of the "Kil-deer," (Kildee, but now spelled as we used to call it, Kildeer) was a little depression on the top of one of the ridges. It did not even scratch out a nest, but found one that suited the purpose and laid its eggs. They were so keen of sight and so quick on the wing that they could dodge either finger stone or shot. It was thought a feat to shoot one, and I never heard of but one being shot. At the flash of a gun, so quick were they, both in sight and wing, that they would get out of the way before the shot reached them.

I have omitted one item of spring work, the whitewashing. There was no limestone in our section, and we depended upon oyster shells for lime. We would build a fire of four foot firewood from the woodpile, with a solid bottom of large sticks, and build it high enough to hold all the shells, and set it on fire, when the shells would be burned into a beautiful white lime with which we would whitewash all the walls that needed it, which was usually all those below stairs, and board fences and gates around the house.[40]

*Scraping up the threshed grain came after harvesting. Drawn
from tools owned by Thomas E. Taylor.*

After mowing came harvesting, the corn having been plowed as it needed it and "laid by" [*i.e.* plowed for the last time]. The reaping machine had not been invented, and so we used the cradle, that having taken the place of the sickle. The wheat or rye was bound into sheaves and put in shocks of a dozen sheaves each. The children were nearly all, boys and girls, kept from school to carry sheaves for shocking.

We always needed extra hands in harvesting, and one of my uncles had usually four or more hands at work in his shoe shop who were always ready and willing to help us. All the mechanics in the neighborhood worked in the harvest fields. The rule was, to pay them the wages per day that wheat sold for per bushel. If wheat was worth a dollar per bushel, they got a dollar a day; if wheat was a dollar and a half a bushel, wages were a dollar and a half per day. If a farmer was a little slow in harvesting, so that his wheat got too ripe and it "shattered" in cutting, some of his neighbors who were done, would help him out.

About ten o'clock in the fore-noon the women would take to the harvest field a liberal lunch, which we would eat in the shade of a tree or at the fence corner. In that lunch we always had what we rarely got at any other time, chocolate. We had it for two reasons, it was a delicacy and it kept hot longer than coffee. While we did not need any thing to keep us warm, chocolate, as well as coffee, is better warm than cold. The chocolate which we used was Walter Baker chocolate, in large cakes. The Cocoa used today was not known.

The farmers in that section bound their sheaves as large as a "double band" would make. In some sections of the country, it has been customary to bind sheaves with a "single" band—that is, with a band of a single length of the straw, with two men to "take up" after a cradle. With us they would have been but "half hands" and paid but half wages. We bound the sheaves as large as a "double band" would make; that is the binder would take a bunch of wheat in his left hand, near the heads, with the right hand divide it in two parts, and by a dextrous turn, twist the two together so that when applied to the sheaf, it would hold fast. When the two butt ends were drawn together and twisted, and the end tucked under the band, the sheaf would stand a good deal of handling without damage.

> When he was in his teens, A.M.J. cradled wheat and bound the sheaves in this fashion. At the repeated urgings of his father, he cut a swath around the margin of the field, salvaging the grain that the horse-drawn binder would otherwise have mashed down on its first pass around.

My uncle, Mahlon K. Taylor, who was an expert cradler, did a days work which was thought to be remarkable. We had a field of about fifteen acres of good wheat which stood very even and straight, and he concluded he would see how much he could cradle in one day. We went to work one morning after breakfast and worked ten hours, from seven till twelve, and from one till six. The next morning we shocked the wheat, and found we had just one hundred twenty five dozen. With good wheat, we always expected a bushel of wheat for every dozen sheaves, [*i. e.* for every shock of 12 sheaves]. The great day's work soon became noised abroad; and for some time afterwards neighbors would call to find out if what they had heard was true. There was no doubt that we had cradled one hundred and twenty five bushels of wheat in our day of ten hours.

While I was active, I had not strength enough to do a full days work of that kind and I only bound the sheaves after a raker.

Farmers "topped" their corn. When it had got its full growth we cut off the stalk just above the ear, and after the blades had wilted, when the dew was on in the morning, we bound it in sheaves, and fed it to the sheep in the winter. In doing so, I have many times found the sheep in the morning covered with snow, and huddled together.

When the corn was ripe and dry, we husked it. We did not cut it up as is very generally done now. We sometimes "pulled" it; that is, when the corn and husks became dry, drove the wagon along a row and pulled the ears from the stalks, and hauled them into a "corn heap" near the barn, and husked them, saving the husks for the cows. If we husked the corn on the stalk, we let the cattle in the field while the ground was frozen, to eat the husks.

After harvesting was over, we plowed for next year's wheat crop, and when the ground was ready for sowing we hauled all the manure from the barn yard ("cow yard") and the hog pen, usually a good supply, and scattered it over the poorest part of the field. The farmers knew nothing of any artificial fertilizer except Plaster of Paris, which they sowed on clover.

> The application of lime and plaster of Paris, and the raising of clover, were two of the elements that made the Loudoun System of farming a success. The other two were deep plowing and the rotation of crops. Combined, they had restored the Taylor farm until, as John wrote earlier, it was no longer "very poor, but by careful management it became quite productive" (p. 16).

We had not yet heard of "wheat drills" but sowed our grain "broad cast." We would take a bag (we did not use the word "sack") and tie the string to one corner so that we could hang it about the neck with the mouth in front and about a bushel of wheat in it. We would catch up handfuls and sow them broadcast having first marked out the field into "lands" of a proper width. A little practice enabled one to sow it very evenly. We then dragged a heavy harrow over it. Now a man will do the same work in a better manner sitting on a pleasant seat driving two horses.

Late in the fall, we always had a buckwheat patch to cut and thresh. Almost every farmer sowed some. It was threshed on a "floor" which was simply a small plot in the field where the crop grew, cleaned off smooth and level.

I have always wondered where the name buckwheat came from, and I now learn by the Dictionary of Phrase & Fable that it comes from the German "buche," "beechwheat."[41] If our ancestors had only had the judgment to follow that and given us "beech" instead of "buck" wheat, the name would have had a meaning, for the grains of buckwheat and beech nuts are of exactly the same shape.

After the fall seedling was done we went into the woods and, from the down and dead trees, cut and hauled to the wood pile fire wood enough to last all winter, not less than thirty or forty or even fifty cords. We concluded it best to haul it in without cutting it into cord wood, as was customary, thereby saving the time when we had other work to do, and cutting it up as we needed it, and saving the chips.

During the winter we "trod" out the wheat and threshed the rye. We had a "treading floor" in the barn about 40 feet square. Many farmers barns were not large enough for that, and they had what is called a "threshing floor" in the Bible: a level piece of ground, fifty or sixty or more feet in diameter, made smooth and packed hard.

Threshing machines had not been invented. We stacked our wheat as near the barn as we could, in the "stack yard," and when we commenced treading it out, we would take the sheaves into the barn, take off or loosen the bands, and lay a ring of sheaves four feet or four sheaves wide all around the floor. We laid the first row flat on the floor, the next one with the heads upon the butts of the first and so on all around the floor. We thus had a ring of sheaves about four feet wide, with the heads of the wheat only showing, and a vacant space in the middle of the floor, of about twenty feet in diameter.

We then put four horses, two abreast, walking around on the wheat, against the way the wheat pointed. After the horses had walked around sufficiently, two of us would each take a pitch fork, one on each side of the wheat, and turn it over. This we would repeat until the grain was all out of the straw, which was then raked off and stored as feed for the cows and steers during the winter.

We never fed our cows hay. We messed the milk cows twice a day, usually with wheat bran and chaff mixed wet, and we gave them all the wheat straw they would eat. They ate straw trod by horses much more greedily than they eat that threshed with a machine, because the former was mashed and much softer than the latter.

Treading out wheat always made me feel as if I had a cold, headache, back-ache and slight fever, the result of the dust; and my grandmother used to say it always made me "take a bad cold."

When the wheat was all "trod," or when the floor became full, we cleaned it. We ran it through the wheat fan twice; the first time through, the coarse riddle taking out the chaff only; the second time through, the fine riddle taking out the "white caps," leaving only the clean wheat. A "white cap" was a grain of wheat with the chaff still fast on it. We then took it to the mill, where it was passed to our credit, to be drawn out for use or for market. We cleaned our wheat so well that it was never "docked," as that of some farmers was, that is, a number of pounds per bushel deducted, sufficient to make up for the refuse matter the wheat contained. Our miller said our wheat was always clean, no white caps, nor cheat [weedy grass], nor cockle [burrs] in it.

Farmers rarely if ever sold their wheat. They delivered it at the mill and got credit for it at the rate of sixty pounds to the bushel, and when they wanted flour, they got for every sixty pounds of wheat forty pounds of flour and about fifteen pounds of bran.

The mill to which we went was four miles off, and the head-race was more than a mile long. It would not infrequently become foul, and the customers of the mill would be invited to meet at the mill-dam on a day named, armed with a shovel. We would clean out the race down to the mill and get there, perhaps at late dinner time; and find a scrumptuous dinner ready, and then we would walk four miles home. There was never any backwardness about helping in any thing of the kind. The utmost good-will and kindness existed between all the people.

As can be readily gathered from John's various references to wheat, it was the Loudouner's main source of cash. On his map of Loudoun made in 1853, two decades after John left the county,

Yardley Taylor showed 77 mills of various kinds, of which 30 were flour mills. It was literally true that a farmer rarely sold his wheat, but bills could be paid by a draft on the miller, and the flour that John's family hauled to the city and sold was drawn from the mill against their account. In effect, one banked his wheat with the miller.

At Wheatland, about four miles from John's home, one can see on Yardley Taylor's map a flour mill that may well be the one used by John's grandfather. When the last water ran over the dam, about 1920, it was owned by the editors' uncle, Millard Fillmore Janney.

When there was no pressing work to do we threshed the rye, of which every farmer raised some. That was done with a flail. I presume many children of the present day, 1901, have never seen a "flail." It was made of two pieces, the "staff" and the "suple." The staff was about five feet long, made of some strong smooth wood (we made them of maple) about an inch and a half in diameter, and at the end dressed into a knob, so that a thong could be tied on securely. A suple, or as the dictionaries now call it, a swingle, was made of some heavy, strong wood, usually hickory, about three feet long and two inches in diameter. One end was made flat and a hole through it, by which it could be fastened to the staff so as to revolve around it. By the thresher taking the staff in his hands and whirling it around his head, he could give a heavy blow to the grain on the floor. Hence the term for a severe flogging, "flailing."

Rye was used mainly for horse feed, though many ate a good deal of rye bread. When we commenced plowing in the spring, we ceased to feed the horses on corn, and fed "rye chop." We cut the rye straw in a cutting box, to pieces about an inch long, and mixed ground rye with it for horse feed. This we used all summer, and when the team was on the road with the wagon.

One of our occupations during the winter was to dress the flax, of which we always cultivated a "patch." We "pulled" it when the seed was ripe, bound it in small sheaves, and let it stand in shock until fairly dry. It was then hauled to the barn and the seed beaten off. Then we spread it out thin on the ground to expose it to the dews and rain so as to rot the substance of the stalks, and loosen the woody fiber. During the winter, in fair weather we would break and dress it.

The flax break was made of, say, six one-inch boards six feet long and six inches wide, dressed to a dull edge on the upper edge, and fastened together at each end about an inch and a half apart. Fasten one end into a heavy block, bore a hole in the other for an inch iron rod and fasten that end to a heavy block. Support on each end on strong feet about two feet long.

Take a similar number of oak boards, dress one edge to a dull edge, fasten one end in a block and bore a hole through the other ends. Insert an iron rod through the holes in both parts of the break, so that when you lift the loose part of the break and let it down, the loose part will fit in to the fixed. Take a bunch of flax in one hand, lift the break head, throw the flax across the break, and by repeated blows the rotted stems of the flax would be broken up and the coarser shives shattered out.

It was then to be scutched or swingled. The swingling board was a board about four feet long and a foot wide, fastened at one end to a heavy block, the other end dressed to an edge. The swingling or scutching knife was made of hard wood, hickory or maple, like a Scotch broad sword. Take a bunch of the flax in one hand, throw it across the top of the swingling board, and by repeated blows of the knife, the fine shives would be driven out. The bunch of flax was then doubled in the middle and twisted into a knot to prevent it from getting tangled.

> The scutching knife struck down the length of the fibers as they hung down along the upended board, and scraped off any pieces of stalk. The knot was untwisted, of course, for the next step, but that might be some time in coming.

It next went to the hackle, which was a board a foot long and four inches wide driven full of polished steel spikes three or four inches long. Take a bunch of the flax and draw it frequently through the hackle, and it would be a length of silky, lustrous fibers ready for the distaff.

SUPERSTITIONS

Some farmers (not Friends though, they were free from all such notions) would not sow flax on any other day than Good Friday. One of my uncles [perhaps the non-Quaker husband of an aunt?] living in another settlement, where the notion prevailed, said his father and a neighbor had each selected ground for a flax patch separated by a fence only. They both prepared their ground ready for sowing on Good Friday, but that day proved to be one of a pouring rain. The neighbor sowed his flax seed, but my uncle's father being from home, the boys said they would not sow flax in the rain if it never got sown. Their father was quite angry on his return and did not intend to sow the flax at all; but in a few days, the ground being in good order, and their father being absent again, the boys sowed the flax seed. The result was that they had a very good crop while their neighbor had none worth pulling. It relieved all of them of their superstition.

There was but little of that sort of superstition in our settlement. Farmers generally had an opinion at sun set as to what the following day would be, judging from the sky and the atmosphere [but] the people had no faith in signs and wonders. The ground hog was laughed at and the wet and dry moon was equally in contempt. But there was quite a shadow of belief in witchcraft left.[42] One day as I was walking down the meadow with a farm hand, I saw a piece of what looked like cloth of some kind sticking under a splinter on a fence stake and took hold of it to pull it out. "Don't do that" said the man, earnestly, "a witch put it there, and if you take it out, you don't know what will happen to you."

> The hand was clearly not a Friend, and John obviously saw no need to say that he wasn't. Indeed, if matters stood then as they did a century later, there is no chance that he was. In the 1920's, with one exception, every adult male Friend in the neighborhood was either a landowner or a businessman. The exception managed the estate of another Friend. This set of affairs had its origins during the initial surge of Friends into Loudoun, when they all bought land, either from Lord Fairfax or one of his assignees. It was maintained by Friends' insistence on education and on a way of life which made waste and extravagance impossible.

> About witchcraft: At the time of World War One, our cook conjured a wart from the elder editor by rubbing a bean on it and having him hide the bean, tied in cloth, under the porch of a neighbor.

An old house of which there was one on nearly every farm could remain empty but a short time, without the reputation of being haunted. There was one on a farm adjoining ours, which was believed to be haunted by a great many people, who feared to go near it after night. One summer certain queer noises were heard in it. The noise was varied from a short h o o h o o repeated, to a prolonged h o o o o, with a sort of buzzing sound. Some young men [investigated but] the sound would be heard always when they were not expecting it. If they were on the lookout at the house it would be in the woods a mile off, and if they were in the woods, the sound would lead [to] the house or near it. It left the neighborhood excited for a good while but, when it was explained, it proved to be the work of three young men strangers in the neighborhood.

In October of nearly every year a drove of cattle from Indiana or Illinois would be driven in for sale to the farmers to be fed and fattened during the fall and winter. They would get pasture till they could be sold. Three men had brought such a drove and were selling their cattle, and having heard of this haunted house on an adjoining farm concluded to have some fun. They would take a piece of shingle about six inches long and an inch and a half wide, and dress it to the size and shape of a large knife blade, tie a twine string through a hole in one end, and the other end of the string to a short stick about two feet long. Then by swinging the stick back and forth, it would make what was a not at all pleasant sound to be heard of a dark night by a timid person. By a manipulation the sound could be varied; by swinging it round it could be prolonged indefinitely. After it became known every boy in the neighborhood had his "buzz" as he called it.

Some localities were believed to be haunted. There was a deep heavily timbered ravine just on the east line of my grandfathers farm, which the "big road" crossed. Many of the neighbors were afraid to cross it on a dark night [and it] was known through the neighborhood as the "haunted hollow." We never learned the origin of the title, and never heard of but one ghost in it. There was a grog shop half a mile beyond it at which some of the farm hands would gather on Saturday evenings, Joe McGeth who worked for my grandfather among them, and he would sometimes get quite tipsy. He had a little feist which followed him everywhere, and one evening when Joe had become quite drunk, the "boys" caught his dog and tied all the white rags they could find around him, so that he looked like a big bundle of rags. Just as Joe reached the edge of the hollow he heard something behind him, and looking back saw his dog. With a wild "hellow" he broke into his best gait and kept up his yelling. The folks in the kitchen heard him coming. He came with a yell tramping on the porch, and as they opened the door, Joe fell headlong on the floor. Just as they raised him to his feet his dog came panting in, and then the shouts of laughter brought Joe to his senses. That was the only ghost ever really seen or heard in the hollow.

FARM ANIMALS

We had good stables for the horses, but none for the cows, colts and steers. The cows and steers were in pasture in summer but in winter they were in the "cow yard" (barn yard). There was a projection of the frame of the barn on the south side, of about ten feet, which made a good shelter for a large part of them.

The hogs slept where they could, and on a cold, or specially a windy night we could hear them grunting and squealing at each other as they were being crowded. Sometimes one would come in late, after the rest were close in their bed, and gently lie down on top of and between two, but would finally squeeze himself down between them with much grunting.

The sheep were left in the field without any protection but fed twice a day on "fodder," the tops of corn. My task as a boy was to feed the "stock" hogs: that is, the hogs which we were not feeding to kill: and feed the sheep. The hogs "ran out." I would go to the corn crib, get my arms full of corn, and call out "p-o-o-o-e, p-o-o-e" a few times so that it could be heard all over the farm. If the weather was fair and not too cold, and the hogs were in the woods, nearly half a mile off, rooting about in the dead leaves, you could see a hog, at the first sound of my voice, stick up its nose and ears, and with a huh! huh! start at full gallop towards home, followed by the whole drove, grunting out its huh's every few jumps.

Every farmer had an "earmark" for his hogs, so that when they "ran wild," as they nearly always did, they could be known. My grandfathers mark was a "full crop" off the right ear, and two slits in it, that is, the point of the ear was cut off and two slits cut in the ear; and a "half crop" off the left ear; that is, only half the point was cut off.

In 1938 W.L.J. recorded the memories of an old cousin about the Civil War. Cousin Charlie remarked, "Mosby knew every pigpath everywhere," meaning he was familiar with the local terrain. Pigs obviously continued to wander unpenned for some decades after John left Loudoun. And not only pigs: As late as the 1930's the Lincoln blacksmith was still letting his cow wander loose on the county roads, bringing her in every evening for milking, often after quite a hunt. His first stop on the search would be at our father's store, to see if any of the customers or loafers knew which road she might be on.

Some farmers, after shearing their sheep, marked them with a "tar stick" with their initials, but we did not mark ours, because we never let them "run out."

Our call for the cows, if they were at a distance, was "sookey, so-o-o-ky." The call for the horses was "cope, co-o-op," and that for the sheep "mee, me-e-ech," and that for the fowls was "chick, chick, ch-i-c-cky." In other parts of the country, they have different calls. In New England about 1850 the call for horses was co-jock or co-jaw; that for cows bos, bos, or koh; for sheep, prolonging the last syllable, ca-naan; their hogs were kept in.[43]

Every farmer had, besides a small flock of geese, one of turkeys, and a large number of chickens, but the improved breeds of fowls now so common were not known; they were simply geese, turkeys, and chickens. The same was true of the cattle and hogs, there were no improved varieties. Some farmers had some merino sheep, but ours were simply sheep. A good deal of care was given to the improvement of horses: two kinds being popular: the Royalty, a dark iron gray, and the Chester Ball, a light-sorrell; both good, serviceable farm horses.

Our fowls were never specially fed; the geese and turkeys getting their living when the stock hogs were fed, and in the cow yard; and the chickens off the wheat stacks and straw pile, and in the fields in summer. They had no shelter, and all but the geese roosted in apple and other trees. None of them were regularly fed, except when specially fed to fatten for market. A few weeks before Christmas we put about a dozen geese in a pen with running water through it: and fattened them, and sent them to market with the hogs. A fat goose on the table was not very common.

In the spring, when the geese began to shed their quills and feathers, they were driven into a stable. The "cutting room" (the room along side the stable in which we cut the straw for feed) was swept out, and the women picked the geese and pulled the quills which we needed for pens. Steel pens were not known. The feathers were used to keep the beds and pillows well filled. We all slept on feather beds, if the supply was sufficient, and if not, the boys and men slept on straw. I have tried all kinds of beds, from the board floor to the best springs and mattresses, and I have never found any thing more satisfactory than fresh oats straw.

A hundred years later, at least some boys in the neighborhood were still sleeping on mattresses stuffed with straw. With all deference to John's opinion, how lumpy they got!

My uncle built a new smoke house and moved the old one near the corn crib, and let the hogs have the ground floor and the chickens the upper. I feel very sure we treated our stock and fowls as kindly as any of our neighbors.

Almost every farmer had a few hives of bees. The hives were merely boxes made out of rough oak boards. Some were made of straw as door mats are now made. If honey was wanted a hole was dug, not quite so large as the hive and about six inches deep, some sulphur set on fire, put in it and the hive set over it, and the bees all killed, thus destroying a whole swarm of bees for a few pounds of honey.[44]

The road wagon needed "greasing" with tar.
Drawn from a tar bucket owned by Thomas E. Taylor.

EQUIPMENT AND TOOLS

The wagons were not the light, uncovered wagons of today, but a well made bed that would "bed" from twelve to 16 barrels of flour, with oak bows supporting a cover. We had but one wagon, a four horse one with a bed neatly and strongly made, with the front and rear ends leaning outward so far that it was difficult to get in the wagon over the front gate. The favorite color was blue, Prussian blue being the most durable color. When we wished to use the running gears of the wagon for hauling stones, wood, manure or other things, we hoisted the road bed up in the wagon house and put on what we called the "wagon bed," made, bottom and sides, of loose planks, such as those used on the streets today. We had no light, well made two horse wagons as we see every farmer have now.

Farmers "greased" their wagons with tar, some of them mixed grease with it. I have seen a wheel that had been greased with tar only, refuse to turn, after having stood long enough for the tar to cool and harden, it having been heated so as to be turned into pitch.

Every farmer had a barrel of tar, and there was kept on top of it some water, so that "tar-water" could be had as a medicine. It was used for many ailments. It is said to have been discovered by Bishop Berkeley, who wrote a treatise upon it, and praised it very highly.[45]

The plows (we spelled it plough then) were good. They were what is known as a colter and bar share plow and were different from, and much heavier than any plow of the present, unless it may be the sulky plow. A modern plow would hardly turn the blue-grass sod we had to plow. The cabinet maker in the neighborhood made the furniture and farmers plows and harrows. Mr Randy a farmer was handy enough to make his own.

> We have already met the formidable cabinet maker Gideon Davis, and shall meet him again. John's memory that Gideon Davis "made nearly all the plows used in the neighborhood" (see p. 14) is verified by Yardley Taylor, a nurseryman, mapmaker, and geologist-historian of Goose Creek. In 1854 Taylor, remembering his youth, wrote a correspondent: "Benjamin Bradfield, then of this neighborhood, brought a mould board from Pensylvania about 1808, and had a plough made to it. An ingenious ploughmaker here, named Gideon Davis, seeing the mould board and believing it to be too small for our purposes, soon made a pattern for a larger one, and had some cast and tried and they soon came into general use." (From p. 80 of the best history of Loudoun County yet produced, *From Frontier to Suburbia*, by Dr. Charles P. Poland, Jr.) From John's testimony it would have been quite possible for a Goose Creek farmer to stop plowing with one of Gideon Davis's plows, go back to his house,

built by Davis, thereupon die on a bed made by Davis, and go to his grave in a coffin made by Davis, carried in a wagon likewise made by the same indefatigable man! Gideon sired a family that rendered similar services to the area for more than a century. Of a later Davis it was said that he could fix a steam engine—or a bodkin.

Our shovel plows for plowing corn we made ourselves, at least my uncle made his, and he made his harrows and his sleds.

The hay or pitch forks were made by the neighboring black smith and were not made of steel, but of iron, and were very heavy and inconvenient, with tinings thicker than your thumb! The manure forks were also home made and were so heavy that an empty one was enough for a boy—three or four prongs, some flat, an inch wide, and the round ones as thick as a man's finger. The first steel forks ever seen in the neighborhood were the load of a pedler. They were quite a curiosity, but were soon in use.

Our axes were made by the blacksmith, were not such as are now used, and cost nearly three times as much. If we needed a screw and nut, or a staple or rivet, we had to go to the blacksmith and have it made; or a hammer or a hatchet, they too must come from the blacksmith shop; and cost two or more times as much as they cost now at the store and not near so good.

Our brooms were made by the negros, first by an old man who had become so decrepid as to be worthless to his master; he was unable to work on a farm and his master allowed him to go where he pleased. His wife (so-called) was owned by our nearest neighbor, and he made his home there and made brooms; but a young man who lived with us learned to make brooms, and made much better ones than "Old John Lucas" made. He made them with oak splints instead of wire, as now.[46] He also learned to make a very superior splint basket. I saw one when last in Richmond, Indiana, still in use, which he made for my mother more than eighty years ago. Farmers always raised enough broom corn to make their own brooms.

FURNITURE

Our furniture was made by the cabinet maker of the neighborhood. The best was made of wild cherry and polished with beeswax. Varnish was not used on furniture. The wax was melted on to the wood and a warm flat iron passed over it, and then it was rubbed vigorously with a woolen rag, which produced a bright polish. On Saturday the furniture, the bureaus, grandfathers desk and bookcase were inspected, and those that needed it were rubbed and repolished. If the polish had become defaced, we melted a little wax on the rag and restored the polish by vigorous rubbing.

The bed steads were all corded, that is, the rails were bored with half inch holes, about eight inches apart, through which bed cord was run each way. We had one bed with a sacking bottom, which came to my grandmother at her marriage. Instead of holes in the rails there were pins. The bottom was made of heavy hemp sail cloth, with eyelet holes worked near the edge, by the aid of which and the pins in the rails the bottom was stretched tight.

In almost every house there was a trundle bed in which the young children slept, which was made to move on castors or rollers and short enough and low enough to be "trundled" under the parents bed during the day.

We had one household implement which has I believe gone out of use entirely, the warming pan. It was made of brass, about a foot in diameter, with a hinged lid, and handle four or five feet long. To use one, fill it with hot coals, and pass it quickly several times between the sheets just before getting in bed.[47]

I have no recollection of a carpet of any kind. Floors were kept uncovered but scrupulously clean, one means of doing which was frequent scouring with fine sand.

Our furniture was limited. A cherry bureau in each of two bed rooms, a mirror (marked on the back $12, better ones can now be bought for a dollar and a half) in the parlor and one in two bed rooms, a dozen "windsor" chairs,[48] and my grandfathers book case and desk, known in colonial days as a scrutoire, were about the whole, with a cherry table in the parlor.

In every Friends house you might find a "sampler" framed and hung in a conspicuous place in the parlor. Every girl worked one. It was worked on an open canvass with silk and commenced with the alphabet in Roman capital letters, which were followed by the alphabet in common type. In the center was a tree or bird or some ornament, and at the bottom the name of the owner. Many of them have descended as heirlooms.

There were no photographs nor no portraits except painted ones, and they cost too much for farmers. The only thing of the kind was the "profile," which was made by an apparatus that gave an exact side view of the face; and when the picture was made on white paper, was neatly cut out, and the paper framed on something black, it gave an exact side view of the person; now called a "silhouette." They were very common.[49]

A candle might burn a chair back

LIGHTING

The only lights we had were the kitchen fire, lard lamps and candles. The fire usually gave light enough for kitchen work, but for sewing, knitting or reading we used candles or lamps. To make a lamp, we would take a saucer, an earthernware one with a lip, which were made for the purpose, and coil a wick of coarsely spun tow or cotton or a strip of loose cotton fabric in the bottom of the saucer, with the end just up to the edge, fill the saucer with grease, the drippings from cooked meats were used, and it would give a light sufficient for sewing, knitting, or reading.

If a light was wanted in sickness to burn all night, a saucer was filled with grease, and a piece of paper cut to fit it, and folded from the edge to the center, all round, and the center pinched to a point. This was placed on top of the grease, and the point lighted. It would give a small light all night.

For those who needed a better light candles were used. One would be lighted, and placed on the "candle stand," around which the women would sit and sew or knit, and the men read, except my grandfather, who would have a candle for himself, hung on the back of a kitchen chair by a hook in the top of the iron candlestick. Sometimes when the candle was hung on a lower slat it would set fire to the one above it.

A.M. J. has in his living room the rocking chair of a great-uncle which is burned in just this fashion.

Snuffers have disappeared with candles. There were always a pair, either iron or brass, on the candlestand and there was frequently an "extinguisher," a little tin cone just large enough to slip over a candle and put it out, thus preventing the candle smoke with its unpleasant smell.[50]

We could not buy candles at the store as we can now but dipped our own. To make them, wick was spun loosely out of tow, or cotton wick was bought at the store. We must first see if we had a supply of rods on which to double the wicks. If there was not a sufficient supply I would go into the woods and find some: smooth, straight, about as thick as my little finger, and two feet long.

It usually fell to the lot of my grandmother and myself to fix the wicks ready for dipping. We would take a candle rod, hold it upright between our knees, put the wick round it so as to make when doubled the proper length for a candle, and twist each end separately, so that when put together they would double by untwisting. I improved this method, greatly to the comfort of the candle makers. I took a board about two feet long and six inches wide, and fastened a rod in one end upright, around which we could double the wicks.

We would put about a dozen wicks on a rod, and were then ready for dipping. A large kettle, iron or brass, was filled to within two or three inches of the top with water which must be kept hot; and the tallow put into it and melted. We would then take a rod and dip the wicks into the tallow and hang them on a frame made for the purpose, to let them cool. When we had dipped all the wicks, we would repeat the dipping until the candles were large enough.

We did not understand the business as well as the candle-makers of today do. We kept our tallow too hot. It did not adhere to the wick as it would if cooler.

We knew nothing about the moulded candle of today, but there was one mould at our house. It was made of tin, and about four feet long and an inch and a quarter in diameter. The candle it moulded was always cut in two and made into two candles, which would light a large table or room completely. Ours was the only one in the neighborhood, and was frequently loaned on special occasions, weddings and other such gatherings.

SOAP

Soap making was one of the unpleasant labors of the women. The ashes were saved by keeping them from the rain and snow, and in the spring they were put into the ash hopper and kept supplied with water. As the lye ran off, it was preserved until enough was had for a kettle of soap. They would nearly every spring make a barrel of soft soap besides a quantity of hard soap. The soap grease from the kitchen had been saved during the year.[51]

SOCIAL LIFE

Among the events of the neighborhood were "huskings" and "raisings."

Many farmers "pulled" their corn, hauled it to a convenient spot, and made a long pile of it, about six feet high and ten or twelve feet wide. Generally on Saturday night, all the neighbors within two or three miles would meet for a husking. They would take their places along the pile, every man taking about two feet, the aim being to see who could husk his way through the pile soonest. White and black, slaves included, worked side by side. There was always a rather free supply of whiskey, the bottle being passed from man to man: care being had not to pass it too frequently, because there were always some who would drink too much.

If there were negroes enough, as was almost always the case, they would sing a "corn song": and I can recall nothing that I have ever heard which I would rather hear than a gang of negroes singing a corn song. One who had a gift in that line would act as leader. He would mount the pile and improvise; the rest, [and] many of the whites, joining in the refrain. Occasionally, the leader would select someone in the crowd, and improvise at his expense, and would frequently make good hits.

I cannot recall a corn song, but they were like the following, which they sung after their freedom:

> No more peck of corn for me,
>
>   No more, no more
>
> No more peck of corn for me,
>
>   No more, no more.

or to put it in their dialect:

> No mo' peck o' co'n fo' me
>> No mo' no mo'
> No mo' peck o' co'n fo' me
>> No mo' no mo'
>
> No more drivers lash for me,
>> No more, no more.
>
> No more pint of salt for me
>> No more, no more.
>
> No more hundred lash for me
>> No more, no more.[52]

I have heard their united refrain, drawn out into a long shout, two miles off on a still, frosty night.

When the husking was done, a sumptuous dinner was ready: roast turkey, roast beef, pumpkin pie, apple pie, and every thing a thrifty farmers wife could supply; with mush and milk in abundance for all who wished and nearly all ate it.

A tradition was current in the neighborhood about a man living there who, when a boy, was fond of pranks at others expense. Their dining room was a cabin, and as in many cases, there was no floor overhead, only some loose boards and poles. At a husking, just as supper was ready, and a big wooden bowl of mush was placed on the table, some disturbance was heard overhead, and the boy came down with a shriek and sat exactly in the bowl of hot mush.

There was nearly always a negro there with a banjo, who would play and others dance. In his absence, at intervals a negro with a leather apron on would "pat Jubor" by patting time on his apron and with his right foot, while one or more danced. At first the time and the dancing would be moderate, but they would both increase until the hands of the patter and the feet of the dancer would fly so that you could not follow them. When the dancer gave out, he would stop with a "sh-e-uh." Sometimes two or three would join in the dance.

> "Juba" is dancing to rhythmic patting. The name had died out— and
> the practice almost so— in the editors' youth, but at least we learned
> the rudiments of the fast patting of hands on thighs and chest.
> Harold Bell, shopping at our father's store, would pat time for his
> own buck-and-wing dancing.

House and barn raisings were similar events. Frame buildings were
built then very differently from those of today. Now a frame house, no
matter how large, is built with no timber heavier than a scantling two by
four inches; then such a house would have beams six or eight inches
square, or for a barn, a foot square; and it took a good many men to
"raise" one. They went in the morning and at noon had a sumptious
dinner. The whiskey bottle was passed as at a husking, and at a public sale
it was passed too, not alone because of the custom, but because it made
the people bid more freely if they were a little mellow.

> It "took a good many men" to raise a house or barn because the
> beams they used then were not only larger in cross section, as John
> points out; they were also much longer than those used today. The
> uprights extended the entire height of the building, instead of only
> from floor to floor, as in the present-day "balloon" construction.

One amusement of the pioneers of the county was not entirely out
grown, the shooting match. A man would have some turkeys which he
wished to dispose of, and would send out word that he would have a
shooting match on a certain Saturday afternoon. He would put up a
turkey for eight or ten shots (at a mark, not at the turkey) at "nine pence"
(twelve and a half cents) a shot. The best shot took the turkey: the owner
getting a dollar, or a dollar and a quarter for his turkey and the winner
getting it for twelve and a half cents. One turkey might furnish amusement
for the whole afternoon. The winner might put it up again, in the same
way. There was nearly always someone present with whiskey and ginger
cakes to sell. One negro woman, Betty Spence, was known all around for
her ginger cakes. She made two kinds: one very large one which she sold
for a quarter of a dollar, or a quarter of it for a "fip" (six and a quarter
cents); and a round one like a saucer for one cent. The favorite method of

some men to eat her cakes was to buy a quarter of a large cake, which was about an inch thick, saturate it with whiskey, then eat it.

On Saturday afternoon, at every country store you would find a number of neighboring farmers. They would work all the week, and go to the store to make purchases and hear the news. They would spend the afternoon in gossip;[53] shooting at a mark with squirrel rifles; pitching quoits ("quates"), in which they used suitable flat stones; pitching cents (the old copper cents, nearly as large as a half dollar), and pitching half dollars or dollars. No gambling was engaged in, the Quaker influence kept it out. A shooting match came so near a game of chance, that they condemned it.

> As late as 1935 the Lincoln store was still a center of social activity, especially on Saturday afternoons in the summer. A knot of loafers (hard-working men at other times) would be passing small talk on our store porch, and in clement weather one or even two games of horseshoes would be going on down by the blacksmith's shop, where old horseshoes were handy. There was still no gambling—not even the smallest kind of bet.

Pitching a bar, and throwing a sledge (we had no sledge and used a maul) were common, as were jumping, both standing and running: and hop, step and jump, or "half hammer." Wrestling was not uncommon, nor was a foot race.

Horse racing has always been a favorite Virginia pastime, but it never entered our neighborhood. The Quaker influence kept that out also. As an illustration of how far they carried their opposition, a Friend living in a village where there were but few Friends learned that a horse race was to be run in a lane leading into the village, and when the time for the race came, he quietly commenced walking back and forth along the center of the proposed race track, claiming that it was a public highway in which he had a right to walk. He caused them to hunt another track.

One gathering always brought together a crowd, which was not always an orderly one. Friends as well as others were enrolled in the militia but refused to attend the musters, and were fined for not doing so. The musters brought together a motley crowd, many of them of the baser sort, and they rarely passed without drunkeness and personal conflict. The militia was known as the "Cornstalk" or "Flat-foot" militia. One man, who was once a captain of a company, to designate him from another of the same name, was always known as Flatfoot Mahlon Janney. He was a renegade Quaker.

There was but little drunkeness, but every country store kept a decanter or bottle of whiskey, free to all, on the counter. Such an institution as a grog shop was not known. One did exist a mile off, but was abolished before my time.

LAPSES FROM THE STRAIGHT AND NARROW

The preceding paragraph is from the text written the year John died. In the ones that follow, from his earliest version, John remembers a bit more vividly a few who strayed from the paths of temperance.

There were several drunkards in and just outside of our neighborhood. Samuel Iden, a good kind old man, would go to Leesburg about once a month, and come home drunk: and not infrequently have an attack of delirium. A mile away from him was Henry Fredt, a hard working blacksmith, who drank nothing but Port Wine, who came to the store every Saturday afternoon, and got staggering drunk. Two miles north of him was Sam. Rupell, a tanner, who got drunk irregularly but frequently, and two miles east was Conrad Bitzer, a wealthy German farmer, who did not wait for an opportunity to get drunk; and there was "Sukey" Poulson who would ride to Leesburg and always came home drunk.

But the worst case was Edmund Carter. Carter, who had married a reputable widow with four daughters and a son,[54] would be drunk almost every day, and would frequently drive his wife and her daughters out of the house at night, and they would seek shelter at a neighbors. He finally said he was to die, and had his grave dug in his meadow and a coffin made, and at the time fixed he laid himself out in a neat shroud with a cent (an old coinage copper one) on each eye. He laid nearly twenty four hours but finally concluded he was not dead. He then got into a large tub of warm water, and opened a vein in his arm, and when found was nearly exhausted. His conduct finally became so that some of his neighbors took him from his bed one night, and after giving him a severe whipping, tumbled him into his grave, and piled the rails from several pannels of fence over him and left him. He managed to get out before morning, and get to the house. He instituted a suit against some of his neighbors, but it failed, and he finally concluded it was the work of the Devil. It had a good effect, for he behaved himself peacably during the next two years. It has made me have great respect for Delaware's whipping post ever since.

He again commenced drinking, and one evening passed our house on his way home, very drunk. I went ahead of him to a shop where there were several hands and told them Carter was coming home drunk. "Let's give him a coat of tar and feathers." That was agreed to at once. I ran up stairs, snatched a pillow from a bed and threw it out a back window; another went for the tar can, and we started after him; but we did not overtake him until he was too near his own home. One of the company stepped in front of him and accosted him. The rest made their appearance on the side of the road, when Carter asked "What are you going to do with me Jess, you ain't going to whip me again are you?" "No! not now but we give you fair warning that if you get to behaving as you used to, we will give you something worse than the other fellows did, for when we get through with you you'll have the best coat of tar and feathers any man ever had." The threat proved efficient, for he left the neighborhood soon after.

Carter and Iden were the only drunkards that belonged to the Quaker neighborhood, the rest were on its outskirts, three to five miles off.

The neighborhood was an orderly one, much more so than the surrounding ones. I have no recollection of a theft or crime of any kind. An attempt to rob a store about four miles off was made, and that is the only attempt at theft that I can recall.

There was a man, a white man, who lived just on the outer edge of our settlement, who had the reputation of being a "smoke-house thief." He kept his family supplied with bacon from his neighbor's smoke houses, but he was finally "converted" and joined the baptist church. The church was near a mill pond, and the dam just at the head of the mill race, was used for baptizing converts. The story told by the boys was that when the thief was baptized, the water in the race was covered with grease all the way to the mill. He did quit stealing.

"Tricks" were sometimes played. On Christmas eve young men would gather at the stores, where egg-nog would be plenty, and on their way home, they would leave evidence that they had been there. One morning we found our big farm sled, instead of in the tool shed, on top of the roof. At another time we found a big, heavy harrow hanging on a limb of a large black oak tree, twenty five or thirty feet from the ground, in one of our fields. That we found out belonged to Whitson Birdsall, who lived more than a mile off, and some time afterwards we found his "gig," in which he rode to meeting, hid in an alder swamp in our meadow. He was an eccentric old man, who had the reputation of having been an active Tory during the revolution, furnishing supplies to the British army at Philadelphia, and the boys took delight in annoying him.

Neighborhood tradition also charged him with having found some of his neighbors sheep in his field. He claimed them as his own: and if a boy saw him coming, he would hide, and as the old man came along would call out "ma-a-a, ma-a-a."

MORES

I look back to one practice with a good deal of wonder. Farmers would work all day, no matter what they were doing, in the harvest field with the wheat covered with red rust, or treading out wheat in the dust, and go to bed at night and sleep in the shirt we had worn all day; and we would do that all the week. We bathed, or "washed" our faces and hands; and there was a bucket on the porch in which we washed our feet before going to bed. There was no water in which a man or boy could swim nearer than three miles; and bathing and cleanliness of body seemed not to be highly valued, by the men at least.

> In the Bancroft Library manuscript, John adds "and the women I am sure used no night clothes." Neither sex, then, had special nightwear.

> The institution of the Saturday-night bath was still in force a century later. Water that had been pumped by hand had to be heated with wood cut and split by hand. It was then poured into the tub that had been set in position in the middle of the kitchen floor. The order was invariably first the children, then Mama, and last Papa, using different water, of course. And we were still wearing our clothing for a week, including shirts and underclothes. (They had to be washed by hand too, and with homemade soap.)

Among the slaveholders and those living in their vicinity, every thing that could be, was kept locked up. The mistress of the household would have a bunch of keys at her side, and so far did that go, that on a visit to a friend, a non-slaveholder, who was living with his daughter only, she came to him several times while I was there and asked for the keys. Every thing eatable about the house seemed to be locked up.

At the time of the Southampton or Nat. Turner's insurrection, such dread overspread the country that in a neighborhood adjoining ours, as in all other slaveholding neighborhoods, patrols were organized, which patrolled the country every night for some time afterwards. In one case a calf had been killed and left hanging all night to cool. Seeing it, the patroll challenged, and the calf not answering, they riddled it with bullets and buckshot.

I was at the time given the name of a woman, living but a few miles from us who said that she never went to bed without the fear that they would all be murdered before morning and their property burned: and that was two hundred miles from the scene of the disturbance.

In our neighborhood, among the Friends, there was no fear nor uneasiness. The patrols sent out were really more dangerous than the slaves.

THE MEETING HOUSE

The meeting house was two miles off, and nearly all the family went to meeting every "First-day." We had an old-fashioned carriage with three seats for six passengers with the door in the rear. Going to meeting was a great cross to me. I was required to go, but the meetings were not interesting to me, and I never had any person try to give me a reason why I ought to go. I was just required to go.

> "First Day" meant Sunday in the "plain language." The entire
> Taylor family seems to have been active in Meeting affairs, especially
> John's uncle, Mahlon K., Jr., who was a "weighty" Friend—that is,
> an influential one.

We did not have the reverence for Sunday that some settlements had. Friends went to meeting every First Day, but the afternoon was frequently spent in social visits by the grown members of the family and in play by the younger.

There was no other meeting house nor church within four miles, and only one, a baptist, less than five miles off.

I did not know of any church without a fire, as the New England churches were; but there was one Friend's Meeting House in which the

John's Meeting House, still in use.

only fire was on a brick hearth in the center of the room, on which a fire of charcoal had been lighted, and when the meeting convened there would be about a bushel of red hot charcoal.[55]

DEATH

There were no "cemeteries," we did not hear the term. There was a "grave yard" at every church. The one at Goose Creek Meeting house was used by all classes. Friends did not allow monuments or ornamental tombstones. A plain slab, got from the nearest quarry, with the initials and date of death, and sometimes of birth, rudely picked in with some domestic tool, were all that was allowed. When I left the neighborhood (in 1831), there was but one stone of a different sort. It was a small white marble slab, about 2 ft. high, neatly dressed, with the name, date of birth and death of Mahala Updike neatly cut on it. She was not a member, and the propriety of allowing such a stone to stand was a troublesome question with the Monthly Meeting for a good while.

They have passed beyond that, for the last time I was there, there were a good many neat marble tomb stones standing; one about four feet high at the grave of Samuel M. Janney, a very prominent minister of the Society, which had his name and the date of birth and death neatly cut on it.

When the friends and acquaintances of the deceased met at the house, or at the grave, if any person felt called upon to do so, he or she could address the company or offer prayer; but they had no ceremony at the grave, nor no funeral ceremony or service of any kind. It was customary, at the death of a prominent member, to meet at the meeting house, have a "sitting", and there was usually something said there, which all were free to do.

In one respect the practice was wholly different from the present. Those present stood by the grave until it was filled up and neatly patted into shape at the top, and wooden markers put at the head and foot.

In some Friends' grave yards, graves were in a row, without respect to families; in others, as in ours, families were buried together; but many Friends seemed to have but little thought about the bodies of their dead friends. As an evidence of that, I went into the grave yard one day with a quite intelligent relative and expressed a wish to see where so many of my ancestors and relatives lay; but he could not tell me; though he had lived in sight of the grave yard many years. I knew the locality in which they laid, but I found that while the grounds were kept in good repair, the head stones and foot stones of my friends had been allowed to fall down, and had been removed and had been all mixed.

> In the late 1920's, when the editors were young men, after a good deal of discussion all the footstones were lifted up and simply laid aside in piles. At about the same time, it became necessary to stop digging new graves in the older section of the graveyard (which went back to the mid-1700's), since so many old graves were being disturbed by the new ones. The original wooden markers were long gone, and the oldest grave sites could not be distinguished at all. As John makes clear, Friends have historically been more concerned with living than with dying.

There was no hearse in the neighborhood. The coffins were made by the "Cabinet-maker," who made the furniture and wagons (except the "road" beds), and built the houses and barns. He carried the coffins before him on his horse to the house, and they were carried to the grave yard in a four horse or six horse wagon with the cover on.

We had no "burial cases" such as are so expensive now, but plain "coffins," made of wild cherry and polished with bees-wax. Many of the young people of the present day have never seen a coffin. They were made in shape as thus indicated:

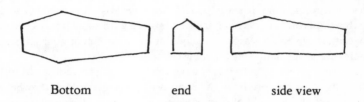

Bottom   end   side view

The top was not flat but like the roof of a house.

Friends used no emblems of mourning, neither in dress, not even black gloves or veils, nor on buildings. On my first visit to Philadelphia, in 1834, I was surprised to see so many emblems of mourning. Their houses were all furnished with solid shutters for the windows, and a large per-cent of the dwellings were kept "bowed," that is, one of the shutters opened about two inches and a bit of black ribbon tied to the shutter, thus making the city appear to be very sickly. I learned it was not because of a death in that house or in that family, but on account of friends who had died no matter where.

While I think Friends were and are justified in their opposition to expensive monuments over the graves and to the memory of the dead, yet the feeling of attachment to the place of their interment is certainly creditable.

Friends were wholly opposed to the customs of New England. There, gloves were sent as invitations to a funeral, three thousand having been sent at one. In Londonderry, New Hampshire, a funeral caused a cessation of business in the neighborhood. Every body quit work, women flocked to the house. Men brought food and the night before was like an Irish wake. All drank N.E. rum, as again the next day, both before and after the funeral. Miss Earle gives the rum bill of one funeral as £6 7s. But that was an Irish funeral, at the opposite pole from the Friends.[56] I have known widows sorely embarrassed by the funeral expenses of a husband.

WEDDINGS

Among Friends there were a few who remained unmarried, both men and women; but early marriages were common. The Discipline of the Yearly Meetings contained specific rules relative to marriages. That of Baltimore Yearly Meeting to which Friends in Virginia belonged had this caution: "We earnestly advise and exhort all persons in membership with us, previously to their making any procedure in order to marriage, to seriously and humbly wait upon the Lord, for His counsel and direction in this important concern; and, when favored with satisfactory clearness therein, they should seasonably acquaint their parents or guardians with their intentions, and wait for their consent."[57]

All persons wishing to marry a person belonging to another Monthly Meeting must procure from the Monthly Meeting to which they belong certificates of their right of membership and clearness from other marriage engagements; they should also procure consent of their parents or guardians; but in the absence of these certificates, the Monthly Meeting may give consent, after mature deliberation. No marriage was allowed sooner than one year after the death of husband or wife.[58]

The first step was a notice read in the Monthly Meeting, as follows: .

"We, the subscribers, purpose taking each other in marriage; which we hereby offer for the approbation of Friends."

A- - - - - B- - - - -

C- - - - - D- - - - -

This notice was read in both men's and women's meetings and a committee of two in each meeting was appointed "to make inquiry concerning the clearness" of the parties "in regard to any other marriage engagements."

If the woman was a widow with children, a committee was appointed "to see that the rights of her children be legally secured." The parties were required to be present at the meeting.

At the next monthly meeting, if the committee reported the parties clear, they were left at liberty to proceed; and a committee of men and women was appointed to attend the marriage "to see that good order is observed."

The marriage always was at a public mid-week meeting at the meeting-house, and after the religious meeting of about an hour, the head of the meeting would announce that the time had arrived for the completion of the marriage of the two Friends present, who were always seated on the womens side of the house. They would then rise and joining their right hands, he would say, "In the presence of the Lord and before this assembly, I take A _____ B_____ to be my wife, promising with Divine assistance to be unto her a loving and faithful husband until death shall separate us," and then she repeated the same promise, substituting his name for hers.

Then a history of the matter, which had been written out by some expert penman of the neighborhood was read, in the meeting, and signed by the parties, and others present as witnesses. This was known as the marriage certificate, and many of them are preserved as heirlooms.

It will be seen that Friends left no room for divorce, and I believe there has been no call for one in the history of the society.

I believe the Indiana Yearly Meeting has omitted the name of the Lord in the contract, inasmuch as marriage is regarded as a civil and not a religious contract.

> Perhaps a few points need clearing up: There was a "women's side" for the couple to sit on because men and women held separate business meetings. After all, the women might have to deal with cases of adultery, fornication, and so on. It is no longer true, unfortunately, that no Friends have ever been divorced. Lastly, John is mistaken in thinking that Indiana Friends had left the Lord out of weddings. About the time that John was writing, the words "in the presence of the Lord" and "promising with divine assistance" occur in the contracts exemplified in the *Disciplines* of Indiana Friends, both "Hicksite" and "Orthodox."

One historian of New England says "Disorderly marriages were punished in many towns; doubtless many of them were between Quakers."[59] "Disorderly" because not performed according to their command.

> 'Twas there, all unveiled save by modesty stood
> The Quakeress bride, in her white satin hood.
> Her charms unadorned by the garlands or gem
> Yet fair as the lily just plucked from its stem.

A tear glittered bright in her dark shaded eye
And the bosom half uttered a tremulous sigh.
As the hand she had pledged was confidingly given.
And the low-murmured words were recorded in heaven.

I've been at the bridal where wealth spread the board
Where the sparkling red wine in rich goblets was poured
Where the priest in his surplice from ritual read
And the solemn response was impressively said

*   *   *   *   *   *   *

But in all the array of the costliest scene
Naught seemed to my eye so sincere in its mien,
No language so fully the heart to resign,
As the Quakeress brides—"Until death I am thine."
                                                    E.C.K.

Probably by the New Jersey poet Elizabeth Clementine Kinney
(1810-1899). Having read the poem, neither of the editors volun-
teered to try to find it in Mrs. Kinney's collected works, if they have
been collected.

What a contrast with a wedding at New London in 1769 at which
ninety two jigs, fifty contra dances, forty three minuets and seventeen
hornpipes were danced and the party broke up at a quarter of one in the
morning.[60]

At a Friends wedding, the special friends of the parties were invited to
a dinner at the home of the bride; and the next day, usually, to a "home
coming" at the house of his parents. The dinner was always the best that
could be furnished; there was no dancing, nor music, nor "unbecoming
behavior" of any kind, and the modern fad of a bridal trip had not been
invented.

The hackle combed the flax for spinning. Drawn from a hackle owned by Thomas E. Taylor.

BLEACHING AND SPINNING

One of the occupations of the women was to bleach the muslin for clothing, and sheets and table cloths. (Cheap table cloths could not be bought as now.) Good bleached muslin shirting could not be had for less than twenty five or thirty one and a quarter cents a yard ("four fips" or "five fips"), and good muslin sheeting, unbleached or "brown," a yard wide cost "three fips," or eighteen and three quarter cents a yard. It was spread on the grass, usually in the meadow, and wet with a "watering pot" (we had not heard the word "sprinkler") while the sun was shining, at frequent intervals during the day. It was thus bleached quite white in a few days.

During the winter the women spent the time not needed in houswork in spinning flax and tow [*i.e.* short broken fibers of flax] on the "little," or flax wheel. Many young persons have never seen a flax wheel. The wheel was fixed to a bench by two posts between which the wheel ran [on an axle], and was turned by a treadle which was worked by the feet of the spinner. A band from the "rim" moved a spindle, which moved the "flyers" and the "spool." The flyers were fitted with a series of wire teeth through which the thread ran and by which it was twisted and wound on the spool. The flax was wound loosely on a "distaff" within convenient reach of and in front of the spinner. This was made with a central post, and four or more arms, starting from the bottom and bent together so as to form a frame. We could make a distaff by going into the woods where we could find on a dog-wood tree a small limb with four branches, in pairs opposite each other, with which we could make a complete distaff by bending the branches together and fastening them to the main stem at the top. The fibers of the flax were fine and silky, and the spinner had a cup of water, usually one end of a small gourd hung below the distaff, in which she dipped her fingers to moisten the flax. She would draw out the flax into an even thread of such fineness as she wished, and wind it on the spool, and when the spool was full, she would put on another.

The thread was then "doubled and twisted" to make a sewing thread or to be woven into table cloths, sheets and towels, or trousers.

They spun the tow into tow thread, which was used either single or doubled and twisted and wove into tow linen, or made into ropes for plow lines, bed cords, or clothes lines, which could not be bought at the store, as they can now. Almost every farmer had a rope walk on which were made plow lines, clothes lines, and bed cords.[61]

In the spring, as soon as the air was warm enough, the sheep were driven to the creek and washed, and then sheared. Our method was to sweep the barn floor clean, tie a sheep's feet together, lay it on the floor, sit down by it and shear it. Some laid the sheep on a bench or table, so that they could stand up. It was one of the most tiresome kinds of our farm work. Shearing six or eight sheep was a good day's work, but an expert Englishman came into our neighborhood. He could take a sheep's head between his knees, and split the fleece down along the back, and with a pair of shears in each hand could shear a hundred in a day.

The wool was then taken to a carding machine, and to do that it was rolled into a sheet and pinned with long thorns from a thorn bush or honey locust. There was a small woolen factory in nearly every neighborhood.

A fulling mill in the community was a necessity. Cleaning and carding wool by hand was a terrible job.

[There] it was carded into rolls about as thick as a man's thumb and about two feet long, and the summer work of the women was to spin it. Wool was spun on what we knew as the "big wheel." It was wholly different from the little wheel. It was made so that the spinner stood, or walked, instead of sitting. It consisted of a large wheel, with a light flat rim about three inches wide, and a quarter to half an inch thick, on which the band ran. The wheel, being about three and a half feet in diameter, ran on an axle, supported on a post set in a bench of the proper height.

The band went over a spindle fixed in a post at the end of the bench. The wheel was turned with a "wheel finger," which was six or eight inches long and three quarters of an inch in diameter, with a knob worked out on one end to catch the spokes of the wheel.

To use the wheel, the spinner would take the wheel finger in her right hand, a roll in her left, with the wheel finger set the spindle to humming, apply one end of the roll to it, catch the wool at the right distance from the spindle to make the thread the fineness wished and draw it out by walking backward. When it was properly twisted, she would wind it up on the spindle. When the spindle became full she would slip it off the "broach," and lay it aside. If the yarn was to be doubled and twisted a broach peg was run through the broach to keep it in shape. A broach peg was made of wood the length and size of the spindle.

Six skeins were considered a good day's work. A skein consisted of four "cuts" of eighty threads of fifty four inches each. This would make 103680 inches. To spin that amount the spinner must walk twice that distance, once in drawing out the thread and again in winding it on the spindle. It makes 207360 inches or 5760 yards, or very nearly three ½ miles. One writer says twenty miles,[62] which is an over-estimate. Girls have spun twelve skeins in a day, but only as an evidence of what they could do.

The yarn, if not woven singly, was doubled and twisted and knit into stockings, or mittens or gloves, and woven into coverlets (of which there was a weaver in every neighborhood) or blankets, flannel, linsey, or Kentucky jeans.

Those who were not spinning in the evening were knitting, making or mending clothing.

They died blue with indigo, red with madder, brown with Walnut or oak bark and copperas, and yellow with annatto, Arnotto, or "aranetta," which [form of the word] is allowable, for the dye comes from the pulp surrounding the seeds of the Arnotto tree.

MEN'S DRESS

Nearly all the clothing of the family was cut out and made at home, except the mens coats, which were cut out by the neighboring tailor, and put together at home.

The men wore low shoes made of what we knew as "upper leather," except the Sunday dress of some men who wore calf-skin boots; or some men wore coarse boots. The tanner classed his skins as "skins," that is sheep and calf skins; and "hides," the skins of beeves, oxen and cows, or horses. The thinner and lighter of the hides were tanned into "upper leather," out of which the uppers of coarse shoes were made; the next heavier hides were tanned into "harness," out of which the "gear," or harness, was made; and the thickest and heaviest was tanned into "sole" leather, for shoe soles.

Shoes worn by men were low, coming just up to the ankle bone. That was the only kind of shoe worn by men. Nearly all had a pair of calf skin shoes for Sunday, and many men had a pair of calf skin boots. We knew nothing of the laced shoe, neither for men nor women.

We all wore woolen stockings in the winter, not any kind in summer. They came up to the knee, and were tied with a garter. Eel skin made the best garter. It was very tough and strong and after use became soft and pliable.

We never used the word pantaloons, nor the inexcusable abbreviation "pants," but "trousers" were usually made of Kentucky jeans, which was made with cotton chain and woolen filling, the filling made of gray wool, the wool of a black sheep mixed with a white one. Almost every flock of sheep had a black one in it, and the wool never fades. Some wore cassinet, or cassinette, which cost about one dollar and a quarter a yard. It was made of cotton chain & wool filling, with a plain twill weave, as the weavers call it. For a better dress some wore "satinet," which was like the cassinet, except that it was of finer material and cost more.

> For all three kinds of cloth the shuttle drew a wool filling across a cotton chain. The jeans and cassinette were twilled—that is, the filling went under one thread and over two. Jeans was the heavier material, cassinette a lighter trousering. In satinet, the softest cloth of the three, the filling skipped over a number of the chain threads, so that the cotton was practically invisible. There was no obvious pattern and the threads, all seeming to flow in one direction, took on a sheen.

Men wore no drawers or underclothing, except a flannel "wrapper" or "wamus," made of cotton and wool, with sleeves, and a waist reaching down to the hips, a jacket and frock coat, and nothing around the neck but the shirt collar. All had gloves or mittens knit by the grandmother or mother, and some had strong buckskin gloves made at Winchester. Men all wore for work days wool hats made by the neighboring hatter. He made "fur hats" also, that is knapped hats, knapped with rabbits fur.

Our shoes were made at the neighboring shops. I wore the first pair of pegged shoes made in our settlement. My uncle was a shoemaker, and a young man, a "tramp jour," came from Ohio who could make a pegged shoe and he made a pair for me. They soon took the place of sewed shoes, except for fine work. Shoemakers could not buy the pegs, but had to make them, but they were soon put on the market.

> In the early 1930's an old store was torn down in Lincoln that in the middle 1800's had been a shoemaker's shop. Upstairs was found a peck of maple shoepegs, looking something like the bamboo needles that used to be used for playing phonograph records. A.M.J. still has on display in his Friendly Store in Lincoln a brand-new pair of leather boots made around 1900, the soles of which are held on by two rows of wooden pegs.

> At the beginning of the second paragraph back, John said that men wore no drawers. That statement flatly contradicts what he said earlier, that women "could not have been induced to wear drawers . . . They were for men's wear." See p. 60.

Buttons were many of them horn,[63] which hot water soon spoiled, or bone. Those for our coats and vests were wood covered with "lasting," which the dictionary defines as a "three-to-seven shaft worsted fabric with double warp and single filling," used for covering buttons and for women's shoes. Women's shoes were also made of prunella, a similar stuff.

> In his *Essay on Man* (iv:203) Alexander Pope plays upon the substitution of the cheaper prunella for sturdier leather in shoe uppers:
>
> > Worth makes the man, and want of it the fellow;
> > The rest is all but leather or prunella.

Men wore two garments which have entirely disappeared though said to be worn in some parts of the country: Sherryvallies, trousers which, instead of the outside seams being sewed, were made with buttons. They were worn while riding in muddy weather, and could be unbuttoned and taken off without injury to other clothing. They also wore leggings for the same purpose. They were usually made of green baize, reaching from the knee to the shoe, and tied at the top with a garter of green "ferret" or "ferreting" [*i.e.* tape].

There was but one man in our settlement who wore a wig. He was not a Friend. The story was told that once, in a violent snow storm, he called on a patient and as soon as he entered the house he was met by the kind-hearted woman, with a broom to brush off the snow, when by an awkward blow she knocked the doctors wig off. She sprang back with a shriek, thinking she had knocked the top of his head off.

Miss Earle says about 1745 every body wore wigs. "A ship load of disreputable, indentured servants who were nearly all rogues, and vaga-bonds were being landed in America, supplied with second hand wigs in order to cut a comparatively respectable figure and obtain positions as school-masters—a calling which seemed to gather the worst dregs of the southern colonies and which was almost always filled by redemptioners."[64] This applies to the southern colonies only: "redemptioners" in Pennsylvania were only poor, not criminals, and came voluntarily. They made a contract with the captain of a ship to take him or her for a fixed price on the condition that they might be hired to some one who would take them for a time long enough to repay the cost of the voyage, sometimes four or five years. Friends always employed a member as teacher, if practicable.

Miss Earle says "By 1716 *** even Pennsylvania Quakers cut their own hair and wore wigs." The emigrants to Virginia did not bring the fashion with them.

"At the beginning of this century women, having powdered and greased and pulled their hair almost off their heads, were glad to wear wigs."[65] With us, while they did not even wear false "switches," they did use hair oils, "bear's grease" being at one time popular.

At one time the fashion was to tie the hair at the back of the head as closely as it could be tied, and it was said of one girl I knew that she tied her hair so tight that she could not shut her eyes longer than a wink.

Many persons feel impelled to hurl their criticisms at the fashions and dress of the day, but our grandfathers and grandmothers make us wonder with what little reference to comfort and convenience they used to dress.

Taylor's bills were light, rarely including more than cutting out or making a coat or a pair of trousers.

The word "surtout" which with us meant a man's overcoat, when used in New England meant a part of women's dress.[66]

We would, very rarely see a man with ruffles on his shirt bosom, but he was always a stranger. Women wore ruffles sparingly.

We did not use either the term vest or waistcoat, we said "jacket." The jacket of the old men was so long that the "flaps" or sides covered the hips, the corners were cut off in front so that it did not button below the waist.

The coat the old Friends wore was precisely such as is worn by every man today, except they had a standing collar and a skirt a little broader.

"Separate" shirt collars or cuffs were not known, nor linen collars. A dress shirt was a bleached muslin shirt. When I went to school in Alexandria in 1830, I bought two "dickies," or "shirtees" which were linen bosoms with standing collars and soon after much worn.

Velvet was common for trousers and jackets; for the former corded velvet or "corduroy" was much used.

Elderly men wore fur hats with wide rims and top boots coming nearly up to the knees, and the tops, some of red morocco, turned down about six inches. These boots were worn with "breeches." Men who wore breeches wore stockings which came above the knees.[67] My grandfather at one time wore breeches, which came to the knee, where they were buckled with a silver buckle, the stockings extending above the knee, lacking only the three cornered hat to justify Holmes:

> But the old three-cornered hat,
> And the breeches,—and all that,
> Are so queer!
> [Oliver Wendell Holmes, "The Last Leaf"]

The shoes were frequently fastened with silver buckles.

Farmers wore for summer use trousers made of flax or tow or for Sunday of "Nankeen," a cotton stuff made of Nankin cotton, of a pale yellow tint, and some old mens were made with feet, so as to dispense with stockings.

WOMEN'S DRESS

Women's dresses were made of "calico" for summer, for winter they were mainly linsey, cotton chain and wool filling, the cotton bought at

Meditating during Meeting for Worship

the store, and the filling spun at home and woven on the family loom, or by a neighboring weaver. Women wore no drawers but a good supply of linsey or flannel petticoats.

Women wore for common use calf skin shoes, made low. Dress shoes were made of morocco.

Sacques were worn, about identical with a boys "round about," except that they were not buttoned.

Young women and girls wore corsets, and some wore them so tight that the wearer could not take active exercise, nor dress herself satisfactorily without assistance. One said to me that when she had no help, she fastened the corset string to a bed post and pulled it tight. Corsets were not kept on sale, but were made at home with a case worked in front into which the "corset board" was slipped, commonly of hickory, finer ones of whalebone. I made a board for a friend which proved so satisfactory that I was called upon to make several for girls in the neighborhood.

"Stays appear in the early inventories of women's attire—as valuable heirlooms." (Earle)[68] In rummaging in my grandmothers bed room closet, I found something I did not know any thing about, and taking it to her and saying "Grandmother, what is this?" "La, if the boy hasn't found my old stays!" They were curiously and wonderfully made of strong Russia sheeting,[69] and supported all round with whale bone and oak splints. I asked her if I might have some of the splints. They provided me with whalebone and oak splints as long as I needed them. I wish I had them as an heirloom.

Tippets for the neck were worn by some, but not of fur. Veils were worn by all women, but the only kind I can recall were made of green barege: a thin cotton and wool stuff. Veils were enjoined by Roger

Williams, and Minister Cotton proved that such wearing was not commanded by the apostles. (Earle)[70]

The pins used were the wire headed ones, the head made of a coil of wire, made just large enough for the pin to fit, and cut into pieces suitable for pin heads, but they frequently came loose. The solid headed pin was not then known. When they came in use, they were not liked. Because the head was not round, the pins would work loose.

The common bonnet worn was the sun bonnet, which was made just as we see it now. It was made with a paste board body large enough to cover the face, and protect it from the sun, with a short skirt. They were made of calico or gingham. Elderly women, who could afford it wore beaver hats, made of fine fur with a crown one or two inches high and a rim six or more inches in width tied under the chin with a ribbon. They were expensive.

For full dress, Leghorn bonnets were worn. Fine ones were quite expensive, costing about ten dollars. I know nothing that illustrates their shape better than a small coal-scuttle turned bottom upwards. They shaded the face of the wearer perfectly. No ornament was worn on them; a band around them and a ribbon on each side to tie under the chin.

The Leghorn was followed by the Navarino, which was shaped just like the Leghorn, but was made of paper like card board; the paper a pale yellow color and stamped, generally with narrow black lines running both ways. They were not long in use.

The calash was at one time generally worn. The best ones were made of green silk which was sewn in wide pleats, into which fine whalebone or wood splints would be run in such a way as to keep the bonnet expanded, or it could be folded together and thrown back on the neck like the top of a "calash" [a light carriage with a folding top] after which it was named, or the top of a modern buggy. Cheaper ones were made of calico or gingham. A poet of 1780 sang:

> Hail, great Calash! o'erwhelming veil
>   By all-indulgent Heaven
> To sallow nymphs and maidens stale
>   In sportive kindness given.[71]

Old women wore caps, but very plain ones, made usually of book-muslin made to fit the head, and with ribbon to tie or two long and wide tabs to pin under the chin.

All elderly "female Friends" wore what was known as a "plain bonnet." It was made of black silk or satin with the front plain like a sun bonnet, supported on a paste-board body, which projected so as to protect the face. The crown was plaited so as to show plaits about an inch and a half wide running from the front to the rear of the crown; it was tied under the chin with a ribbon. Go into a Quaker meeting and you would see the "women's gallery" nearly filled with these somber bonnets, but if you could look into the faces they covered you would see a lot of handsome, bright, cheerful faces.

Rings were never worn by men and rarely by women. Mourning rings were never seen or heard of. Dr. Samuel Buxton of Salem is reported to have left to his heirs a quart tankard full of mourning rings secured at funerals.[72]

Tortoise shell combs were worn, with teeth about three or four inches long, the back two inches or more wide and the comb long enough to reach nearly from ear to ear. They could not be worn with the bonnet, and I have carried them in my hat when on a visit, and handed the comb over on reaching our destination.

Tortoise shell side combs were also generally worn. Some wore curls on each side of the face kept in place by shell combs. The hair was worn twisted into a knot at the back of the head.[73]

Umbrellas were not common. They were made with heavy whalebone ribs. The people seemed not to fear the rain. The usual spelling and pronunciation was "umberrel."

Children were dressed plainly.

AMUSEMENTS

One of the common labors of women was quilting. They did not buy their "spreads" at the store as they can now, but "quilted" them at home. They all had "patch work" covers made of bits of calico cut into pieces sewed together, and spread over a cotton sheet with raw cotton between them, and quilted in squares or sometimes intricate figures. We could not buy cotton batting as now but bought at the store raw cotton and carded it into batts on hand cards such as are now used to card horses, except that they were made with finer wire and were longer. The quilt was stretched on four frames and marked in squares by lines, or if a fine one, by fancy figures of some kind. As it was quilted along two sides, it was rolled up on the frames. When all was ready, the young women and girls in the neighborhood were invited to a quilting, and after a good supper, the "boys" of the neighborhood would appear and the evening would be spent in the plays of the day.

If the quilt was not completed, the mothers would be asked in at another time. Some quilts were made of fine material, scraps of silk from wedding dresses, and were quilted in figures requiring a great deal of careful work. Many of these quilts have descended as heirlooms.

Apple cuttings were common in the fall. They were more for amusement than for business. The men of the farm were asked to bring in a plentiful supply of apples, and those that were ripe were chosen without any other fitness, and they were apt to be very sour. All the young people, boys and girls, were invited to a "cutting." They would seat themselves around a tub of apples, and the boys would pare and the girls would cut the apples: that is cut them into quarters and cut out the cores. When they were done they would eat a good supper, and then engage in plays that were common, in all of which there was singing of some kind of ditty. I can recall only three lines of one of them.

> "Oats, peas, beans and barley grows
> But you nor I nor no one knows
> How oats, peas, beans, and barley grows."

Nearly all, I think all, their plays had penalties which included kissing or some ludicrous performance. A writer of 1744 says kissing seemed to constitute a great part of the entertainment at evening parties every where at that time. The practice had come down to us.

One penalty was for a boy to do some weaving. He must sit on the floor and take the large kitchen tongs and recite some doggerel stanzas; drawing up his knees, run the tongs on the floor under them as a shuttle, and then put his hand on the floor, lift himself up and drop down with a bump. This he must repeat three times as the weavers beam: he must then shoot the shuttle back again, and repeat the bouncing. This must be repeated a certain number of times, the number I do not remember.

One of the penalties for a girl was to kiss a young man "pigeon fashion," each take one end of a string in their mouth and work it into the mouth till their lips met. Still another was for the culprit to go around the room, kiss one and miss one and tell why they were kissed and why they were missed.

DIALECT

The people of the country were almost wholly illiterate, except Friends. Friends had a school near every meeting house, and the children were given a good common school education so far as the ability to "read, write, and cipher" went; but the preceding generation had confined it almost entirely to the boys. I never had any evidence that either of my grandmothers could read or write: and my mother and all my aunts could do either but poorly. The hired help with Friends, both men and women, were almost wholly illiterate. Friends schools kept all the year except two weeks at harvest when the children were needed to carry sheaves in the harvest field.

As proof of the general illiteracy the following were some common pronunciations. "Injins" (onions), "taters" (potatoes), "Pasnips," "sparrer-grass," "cowcumber," "watermillion," "reddish," "currens," "punkin," "pusley" (purslane), and the following "sassafrae," "Laylock," "tother," "furder," "yisterday," "hoss" (horse), "coverlid" (coverlet), "umberel," "ornery" (ordinary), "chist," "skeet" (skate). "Didn't, couldn't, won't, shan't and can't" were all in daily use by almost every one.

I remember that frequently in studying my spelling lesson I would be surprised to recognize a word in common use; in potato for instance: "Why! that means "tater," or ordinary, "Why! that means "ornery!" but in that I was mistaken for "ornery" did not mean ordinary, but meant good for nothing.

We said the hen "sets" and say so yet, for which some over-wise critics find fault, but did our grandmother take a dozen or fifteen eggs and "sit" the old hen on them! She knew better than that: and if the hen "sits" must not the Sun and the moon and the stars "sit" also?

A setting hen was still known as "the old hen" a hundred years later, regardless of her age.

Two words became fixed in my speech so firmly that I have never been able to avoid the improper use of them, "guess" and "reckon." They were in common use instead of "believe," "think," "suppose" or like words. Instead of "I think," or "I suppose," it would be "I guess" or "I reckon," and instead of "I doubt" it would be "I guess not." I find myself using them now at 95 as I did at five. There was a tradition then and it is not dead yet that a Yankee guesses at every thing, but upon asking a native of Massachusetts, he said the tradition was not true, the use of the word was not common. The Friends were all of English origin and emigrants from Bucks county Pennsylvania, so this language must have been of Pennsylvania origin.

The editors don't know about the Yankees, but they reckon John was right about the folks around Goose Creek.

NAMES

At that time but few men, and no women had middle names, hence in families where there were two or more of the same first name, nicknames had to be applied. In addition to that the name was almost always shortened if practicable. There were but few Thomas or William: they were all Tommy or Tom, and Billy or Bill. There were in our settlement "Squire Tommy Nichols," "Swithins Tommy," "Long Tommy," and "Sammy's Tommy." There were "Billys son Sammy," "Swithins son Sammy," "Bacon-fat Sammy," and "Big-bellied Sammy Nichols," and so on.

There were a good many Elizabeths, but they were all known as "Betsy" or "Betty," the Sarahs were nearly all "Sally," the Peters were "Pete," the Williams "Billy" or "Bill" and the Isaacs were "Ike" and so on.[74]

It was very rare that a man or woman was addressed in any way but by their first name; the address was simply John or Mary. Quakers never use Mr., Mrs., or Miss. It was always, not Mr. but John Brown; not Mrs. but Mary Smith; not Miss but Ann Taylor. One of the most annoying things I met with on leaving the neighborhood of Friends was that I was never addressed by my name. It was always "Mr. Janney," and it made me feel as though I was held off at arm's length, as though they feared to make or did not want my friendship. Even now, in my old age, after living fifty five years away from Friends, there is little that is more grateful to me than to be addressed by my name John,[75] instead of "Mr. Janney."

OFF TO OHIO

My mother insisted that I should be a farmer but I told her that I never would be, not that I did not like the work, but I wanted to study, and there was then no inducement for a farmer to study. As it was then conducted, it was plow, plant and reap, just as their fathers had done. If it had been carried on as it is now, it might have had an attraction for me, for at present a farmer must study if he keeps pace with improvements. I was an illustration of the mistakes made by parents. They too often fail to consult the wishes of their children. It frequently happens that the wish of the boy or girl is in the right direction, needing only proper assistance and guidance.

When I became of age I inherited fifteen hundred dollars from the estates of my grandfather Blackstone and my father Thomas Janney. I wanted to use some of that in going to some good school, but my mother opposed it, but did at last consent that I should go to Alexandria to school six months. When I went, I took a letter of introduction to John Pierpont who was teaching there. I went to his school six months studying Euclid, which I could have done just as well at home. My uncle could have heard my recitations and demonstrations just as well as my teacher, who was teaching a common day school of boys from the district, and this when Benjamin Hallowell, a prominent Quaker preacher had a popular boarding school in the city and said to me he could have had me study engineering, which I would have liked. He thought there would be a great demand for engineers, which proved to be true. So I really lost six months and at 21 I was turned loose upon the world without preparation for any of the work it offered me.

Hallowell's school stood next door to the home of Robert E. Lee and his mother. Lee attended the school in 1825, before going on to West Point; that was the same year that Samuel M. Janney, whose tombstone is mentioned on p. 96, studied mathematics under Hallowell. (Hallowell's *Autobiography*, p. 103.) John is right: He missed an opportunity, for Hallowell was an educator of some distinction.

I have written this sketch to cover as much of my life as I intended, but have concluded to add some notes on my later life.[76] By my mothers influence I was thrown on the world unfitted to do any of its business, unless it was daily labor. My uncle Elisha Fawcett was going to move to Ohio and agreed to take me with him. He had a six horse team and what was known as a "Prairie Schooner" a wagon which would "bed" sixteen barrels of flour. Into this his household furniture was packed, leaving room for his sister (my aunt being dead), his sons and us in case of bad weather. We moved about 15 to 18 miles per day, and at night we got a pot of coffee, unpacked our "dinner box," ate our supper, and the men spread their bed on the floor and went to bed.

My uncle bought a farm in Belmont county, instead of going on to Warren county where his brother-in-law and some friends had moved before. He gave me as his reason, that in traveling across the mountains, he had found the coal fires so comfortable, that he determined to buy in a coal county. In telling me this several years afterward, while I was living in Warren county, where we had to ship our coal, he asked me how much I paid for coal. "Eight cents a bushel" I replied. He said it cost him nine cents a bushel to dig it from his own land, so he had made a mistake buying there.

I felt sure I could teach a country school, and the director of a district offered me seventy five dollars to teach a district school six months. I refused, telling them that a man who would agree to teach their school for that would not be fit for the place. I would not do it for less than one hundred dollars, to which they agreed, telling me the school was a tolerably rough one and was familiar with the rod, which I would have to use freely. To that I replied we would see, but I thought not. It had been used liberally by my predecessor.

When I went to the school house on Monday morning and called in the children the seats were all filled, with seventy two boys and girls. I called them to order and told them that I did not intend to have any rules, all that I expected of them or asked of them was to behave themselves properly which I had no doubt they knew how to do. Upon looking up at the ceiling of the room, I saw it was literally covered with "spit balls," little balls of chewed paper shot up with the fingers, not a space as large as my hand without one and many lumps as large as my fist. I looked up at the ceiling and said "I see you have been taught one thing I do not know any thing about and I shall expect you to drop that study." While some of them were amused, many looked very sober. That evening I borrowed a hoe and scraped the balls off clean. I called their attention to the better appearance of the ceiling next morning and said that no more spit balls would be used. The school had but become fairly quiet when I saw a ball fly up to the ceiling and a second one followed it. I laid my hand on the head of the boy who made it, very much to his surprise and to the amusement of the others around him, and pointing to the broom told him to sweep the balls off, "and now remember don't make any more." I never saw another.

I had a quiet and attentive school, with but a single case of punishment. I kept a girl in fifteen minutes after dismissal at night for some impertinence.

I have thought I would have made a successful teacher.

I used nearly the whole of my inheritance in purchasing an interest in a village store, which I did without consulting any of my friends, and which I soon found unpleasant and we separated. I continued it several years, and closed it out with nine hundred dollars in my pockets. I was out of business for several years but found that when the public finds out that a young man is capable and willing, it will find something for him to do. I did all the land surveying needed by sales of farms or subdivision of estates in the neighborhood for several years, and was called upon frequently to write agreements, or papers of many kinds.

I was an active Whig and some of my friends urged me to be a candidate for the legislature to which I consented. I took no part in the contest and was beaten by nine votes in a county convention of about 100 delegates.

I concluded at one time to study law, and bought Blackstone's Commentaries which I read with a great deal of interest. It is admirably written, and very interesting as a history of English Law but I agree with Thomas Carver [?] who said he thought it would be a good thing for America if every copy of Blackstone could be gathered into a pile and burned. It was always the first book put into the hands of a law student, but it is from beginning to end a glorification of the British government and when he is through he thinks it the most perfect government in the world, and hence many of our lawyers are unpatriotic.

In the fall of 1844 I concluded to go to Columbus with our representative, to get a clerkship in the House. I succeeded in securing an appointment. The salary of clerk was the same as members, three dollars per day, and the sessions were usually 100 days. I served as clerk three winters. At the last session, the pay was increased to four dollars per day. I made friends of many of the members which lasted as long as they lived.

One thing which occurred during this last session gave me a great satisfaction. Alfred Kelley had secured his election to the Senate for the purpose of securing the passage of an act incorporating the State Bank of Ohio. It was passed by the Senate, then by the House with amendments which sent it back to the Senate, from which it came back with a long list of amendments, mostly verbal, but Mr. Kelley was very anxious that these amendments should be properly adopted. He asked the clerk if he had a clerk who could read them properly. Yes, he replied, Mr. Janney can do it. I told Mr. Kelley how I proposed to read the amendments. I would read the section as it stood, then read the proposed amendment and then read the section as it would read if the amendment was agreed to. When I was through and the act passed, Mr. Kelley said to me "I am very much obliged to you, Mr. Janney. You did that very well. Very well indeed."

I served as a clerk three years, the last year with E.G. Squier, the author of that standard work on the Prehistoric Races of Ohio.

> Squier is best known today for his books of travels in Central America and in Peru, which fetch handsome prices in antique bookstores.

The next winter the House had changed and voted me out but Sam'l Galloway, secy of state, offered me the clerkship in his office. He was then Superintendent of Common Schools and his office had charge of the land surveys made under the Auditor's office.[77] I did the work in the office and had time to copy the maps and land surveys for several counties. Now there are [blank] clerks in the office which is relieved of the schools and the land records.

As clerk I answered one question put to the Secy of State as Comr of Common Schools, which gave me a good deal of satisfaction. A negro, who owned a farm in Miami county on which he paid taxes had his children ejected from the public schools, against which he appealed on the ground that he paid a part of the school fund and hence, could send his children to the public schools. Mr. Galloway handed me the letter and asked me to answer it, which I did, and he sent a copy of my letter as his answer. It was that his children had a right in the public schools.

A few days after, John Moody, Auditor of [the] State[78] handed me a letter from a different part of the State making the same appeal. I handed him my answer to it, and the next day he said my answer was as good a legal and constitutional argument as any lawyer in the city could write, and with my consent he would send it as his answer.

I served two years as chief clerk, and was asked by Mr. Galloway's successor to continue, but I had been elected clerk of the Board of Control of the State Bank of Ohio, which had been done without my knowledge.

I served as Clerk of the Board of Control fifteen years until the expiration of the charter. There were forty one branch banks, and every branch had a member of the Board of Control, and with two exceptions there was not a member during the fifteen years who was not a gentlemen in the true sense of the term.

At the expiration of the charter of the Bank, I was elected Secretary and Treasurer of the Columbus-Hocking Valley Railroad, in which place I served until Mr. Greene [?] sold out the road. The road was a success from the time of its completion. It paid one twenty five per cent stock dividend, and when it was sold, stock at 50 par sold at 80. It was sold to a syndicate in Cleveland, which entered into one of the swindling schemes that have been so common in "High Finance" since. I served the company fifteen years.

During the thirty years, I had been elected a member of the City Council twice, and was a member of the Police Commission, Board of Health, and Director of the Public Library, the charter of which I wrote and had passed by the Council. I was also Member of the Board of Education two terms. I was defeated for reelection by 23 votes, by a man standing at the poll and charging me with doing as a member of the Board a thing which, a fellow member told him the next day, I was the only Member who did not do it. That is the only case in which I lost any vote when a candidate.

I wrote the ordinance establishing the first board of health the city ever had, and wrote and had passed the rules governing it. Afterwards, when the physicians in their meeting were discussing a board of health, they seemed to be of the opinion that the chairman or president of the Board should be a physician. The young man whom we had as medical appointee of the Board said he was opposed to it. He could name a citizen who would make a better president of the board of health, than any doctor in the city. "I refer to Mr. Janney."

I was secretary and treasurer of the Republican State Committee or State Republican Committee three years, one of them the historical one [1863] in which Clement L. Vallandigham was the Democratic candidate after having been tried for traitorous utterances, and sent south to his friends. He went to Canada, and was there through the campaign, but was voted for by the Democrats with enthusiasm but beaten by 100,000. He was the youngest member ever elected to the Ohio legislature up to that time, being just old enough, twenty one. I was a clerk in the House and he was and always remained a personal friend.

> As a staunch Unionist, John is less than absolutely fair to Vallan-
> digham, who had been "tried" only by a military commission, though
> he was a private citizen. He was candidate for the office of Governor.

I wrote the ordinance establishing the Public Library and Reading Room and it passed with the opposition of two of the leading members [of the City Council] with a vote of 14 to 2, the two opponents both voting for it, since it would pass. One of them finding it would be popular, began to claim its authorship and got the public to believe his claim. The Library has proved to be a great success, and I look back to my part in its foundation with great satisfaction.

At the earnest solicitation of many of my friends I agreed to serve as assessor for one of the wards. The custom was, and still is, to elect assessors who have nothing to do, and in many cases because they are fit for nothing and an examination of their returns shows in many cases their total unfitness. I followed the law as closely as I could, but it cannot be obeyed. It requires many things to be done, which cannot be done in the time allowed, nor in treble the time. I followed or obeyed the law as closely as I could, and the citizens of the ward and others said I was the best assessor they ever had.

After 1883 I had no regular employment, and the health of my wife having failed, my daughter, Mrs. S.C. Derby made arrangements for us to live with them. This we did till her death, and I did till the second of February 1902, when I fell and injured my hip joint, from which I suffered several months, when I was attacked by disease of the kidneys and rheumatism, which have proved so far incurable. I see only so much of the world as passes in sight of my back window.

And now after looking back over my life I realize one great mistake I made. I never, but once, had an ambition of any kind enter my mind. Our reading book at school was Murrays Reader, and they had lessons from the British authors, Goldsmith, Hume, Addison, Steele. I had read at the morning lesson one of the most beautiful, and on my way out to the play ground at noon, I remember the thought passed through my mind "Oh! if I could only write like that." The thought was checked by my reflection that I could not, because those good things were all written by Christians and I am not a Christian. There were two mistakes in my conclusion. The fine writers whom I admired were not all Christians, and I, a boy of 12, could not agree to what I was called upon to believe to be a Christian—so that my boyish ambition to be a good writer was checked. As I soon learned after I became part of the world that all it asks is that you do what you are doing in the best way, that has been my only ambition. And this has been the great mistake of my life. I think no life is, or can be complete, that does not have an end to gain, a purpose to accomplish, some thing to be done in the future.

INTERVIEWS WITH ABRAHAM LINCOLN

My first interview with Abraham Lincoln was in this city [Columbus, Ohio]. He was on his way to New York to deliver what became historical as the "Cooper Union Speech." He had agreed to make a speech here. For some reason I could not be present to hear the speech, but my son, than a well grown boy did hear it, and, when asked what he thought of it, replied, he was not able to say whether it was a good speech or not, but he felt sure that any person who should undertake to reply to it, would have a hard task.

After the meeting Mr. Lincoln was given a reception at the house of Governor Wm. Dennison, to which the public was invited, and which I attended. I waited until the crowd had been introduced, when I presented myself. He grasped my hand very cordially, and said to me "Have you a relative living in St. Louis?" I replied I had a cousin there. He said "Nathaniel or Nat. as every body calls him. He is a dealer in Insurance. I have bought insurance of him, and I can say to you that you have one relative who is a gentleman at all times and under all circumstances." I became satisfied that that introduction to the name of Janney made so favorable an impression on him that the name itself was a sufficient introduction, and needed no endorsement.

The next interview was after his election to the Presidency. I was Secretary of the State Republican Committee, and complaints came to me, that one of the Collectors of Internal Revenue was throwing his influence and patronage in favor of the Democrats. I wrote him but my letter did not improve the case; so having some other business in Washington, I determined to appeal to the Internal Revenue Department. Having no acquaintance with the Commissioner, I determined to ask the President to introduce me, for if I went to the Commissioner as a stranger, the case would be pigeonholed to take its turn. Upon presenting myself he met me cordially. I apologized for troubling him, but upon stating the case to him, all I asked of him was to indorse on an envelope I handed him a request that the Commissioner would hear me on the case. I excused myself for troubling him at all with it, but he replied by saying to me that at any time when I wanted his advice on any subject or matter, not to hesitate for he would be always glad to see me. He wrote across the end of the envelope "The Commissioner will hear Mr. Janney on the inclosed paper. A. Lincoln." I have the envelope now. I handed the letter I had to the Commissioner saying I wished to preserve the envelope. He turned to his secretary and indited a letter to the Collector, which he thought would wake him up and I thought it did, for I heard no complaint from or about him afterward.

I did not see Mr. Lincoln again, until my son-in-law W.L. James, who was serving as Quarter Master General, Army of the Potomac or Army of Virginia, I believe it was, and stationed at Fortress Monroe was suddenly dismissed by Secy of War Stanton. The station was one of a large business, and among other things that made it so was that it was the depository of injured wagons, and army equipment, and worn out or diseased horses, and at frequent intervals the horses would be sold at public sale. They were many of them merely worn out, tired and only needed good feed and care for a few months to be as good as ever. At public sale they would sell at 12 or 18 dollars and with a few months care would be worth 50 to 70 dollars. They must be advertised, and Mr. James noticed a few men always attended the sales and bought the horses, usually for 12 to 15 dollars. A cousin from Pennsylvania was there at the time of one sale when Mr. James suggested to him to buy some of the horses. He said he had no money. Mr. James said he had some money in the bank at home and if he would buy some of the horses, he, Mr. J. would give him a check on the bank at home, and he would feed and care for them till next spring; they would divide the profit. Of this agreement, Mr. James friend made a memorandum, which he put in his pocket, but on his way home he lost it in the street at Washington. The provost guard found it, handed it to the Secy of War, E. M. Stanton, and Col. James was at once dismissed, for violating the Articles of War.

Senator Cameron appealed to the Secretary, but Mr. Stanton never agreed that he was wrong. In a letter from Mr. James he said he [hoped] Mr. Cameron would get him reinstated. I asked him by telegraph if he thought I could be of any service to him by going to Washington. He thought I could. I went at once. The first day was Cabinet day. The next day was used up by calls from Congressmen and other privileged persons, but on the third day I found the ante-room filled with men, women and boys, all waiting to see the President. I had become acquainted with the genial Irish door keeper who said if I would take a seat he thought the door would be thrown open in a few minutes and the whole crowd admitted, which took place. On entering the room, I saw a lounge [*i.e.* sofa], which if I could reach would enable me to see and hear all that was said and done. I sat there nearly two hours, and heard the appeals of men, women and one boy, and the decisions of the President, and among them were the following.

An old woman called with a petition asking for the pardon of her son who had been convicted of carrying percussion caps and medicines which the rebels must have and could not make. A friend of the old lady presented a letter to the President who upon looking at it, said "Lady, this is from Gov. ------------" naming an ex-Gov of Maryland. A man standing by said "Oho, He's dead." "Well suppose he is dead, wouldn't a letter from a dead man be worth more than from a living one!" Mr. Lincoln listened to her appeal, and that of her attorney, and said to her, Madam I am very sorry to hear your story. Your son has been tried by a sworn court, with the testimony of sworn witnesses for carrying percussion caps and medicines across the Potomac to the rebels, things which they must have and cannot buy, and now you ask me to pardon him, through sympathy for you. You will see at once that that offense can not be overlooked, and while it is a very hard thing for me to say, I suspect that if I was to pardon him, it would not be two weeks before he would be doing the same thing, and I am not at all sure, but with your consent and approval, I cannot pardon him.

A woman presented herself. "Well, Madam, what can I do for you?" "I wish to have a pass to Richmond." "Why do you wish to go to Richmond?" "I have a sick sister there." "Hasn't she friends there?" "Yes, but I would like to be with her." "Where are you staying now?" "Baltimore." "Well I have no doubt she will be cared for and I can't give you a pass." She wheeled on her heels and marched out of the room, every fold in her silk dress rustling with indignation.

A man presented himself, and was met with "Well sir, what can I do for you?" Laying a bundle of letters on the table "I wish an appointment as Paymaster in the army." "Oh! I have more paymasters than there is any use for. I need money, more than I need paymasters. I tell you what I would like to do. I would like to trade some paymasters for some money."

He left, disappointed.

A boy presented himself. "Now my little man what can I do for you?" "I want to go to West Point." "How old are you?" "--------" "Oho you are not old enough. You must be eighteen to go there." I pitied the little fellow, he was so disappointed. "What are you doing." "I am fifer in -------- regiment N.H.G. [The dashes are John's.] "Well now you go back to your regiment, and do your duty as I know you will and when you are old enough come to me, and I'll send you to West Point!" The little fellow thanked the President very earnestly, and walked out a head taller than he came in.

I sat an hour and listened to applications and appeals, and it was the most interesting hour of my life. The soundness of judgment and the friendliness of manner with which they were all met and the wisdom of his decisions were so apparent as to force the admiration of all.

I was determined to have the last chance at him for I wished to talk with him. The crowd was finally reduced to two, myself and a good looking girl. She beckoned to me, but I shook my head and she went up to Mr. Lincoln and produced from a pocket, a tablet and pencil, and proved to be a writer. She asked and he answered her questions for half an hour, never intimating any thing but pleasantness. When she got through I presented myself, when he met me with a cordial grasp of the hand, and "Have you been here all this time, why didn't you make yourself known sooner?" My reply was that I was anxious to hear and see him try all those cases, "and let me say to you it has been one of the most memorable hours of my life. That girl will be happier all the rest of her life, from having met the President." After a half hour talk about Ohio, he said to me, "And, now what can I do for you." I stated the case of Col. James, without giving his name, and Mr. Lincoln said "That's Col. James' case isn't it?" Yes. "Well I ordered him re-instated." "Well, it has not been done." "Well now, Mr. Janney, I wish you would go over to the War Dept. and see what's the matter. I ordered him re-instated." I went accordingly and was told they did not understand that Col. James was re-instated, which I reported to the President. He took his pen and wrote a peremptory order re-instating Col. James in his place, and asked me to hand that to the War Department and see if they would understand it. I thanked him most heartily for it, and told him I felt sure he never would forget re-instating a worthy officer, which proved true for Mr. James came through the service with the title of General at its end.

I took the order to the War Dept., handed it to Col. Hardie, who read it, and said "Yes sir. That will be done." "About how soon may I ask?" "As soon as the papers can be made out."

When the President gave me the peremptory demand to re-instate Colonel James, I asked him at what time I should call. "At nine o'clock, I'll be here." Next morning I called, took my seat in the ante-room, which was full of people waiting. As the President came in and went up the steps to his private office, he looked back and seeing me said "Come in Mr. Janney." Every eye in the room was fastened on me with "Who is that to whom the President speaks so familiarly?" I reported from the War Dept. that Col. James would be re-instated "as soon as the papers could be made out." When I left his office two men hailed me and wanted me to help them, were willing to pay me but I begged off that I had managed my own case, but could not undertake another. I had no doubt but I could have had a good fee.

That was on Saturday. I went to Philadelphia that day and reported to Col. James (who was my son-in-law) and Monday mornings mail brought his re-instatement and he went back to his former position. I beat Stanton, who though an efficient officer was a domineering tyrant who deserved to be knocked down many times for his insolence.

> Though John calls his son-in-law "Quarter Master General," there was only one such post and James did not fill it. William Levis James, born in West Chester, Pa., enlisted with other Pennsylvania volunteers in November 1862 at the age of 29. He was an assistant quartermaster, with the rank of captain. On December 8, 1863, he was dismissed the service, but the dismissal was revoked on August 30, 1864. In 1865 he rose rapidly through brevet major and brevet colonel to Colonel and Chief Quartermaster, Department of Virginia. In early 1866 he became a Brevet Brigadier General and was honorably mustered out as of July 31, 1866. In 1880 he is to be found a responsible citizen of Philadelphia, in shipping. (Data from Francis B. Heitman's *Historical Register...of the U.S. Army*, Washington, D.C., 1903, and from the Records of the Office of the Quartermaster General, record group 92.)

I had and have no doubt that Mr. Lincoln's acquaintance with Nat Janney in St. Louis fixed in his mind a very favorable estimate of the name Janney. Upon one interview with him he said to me "Are you a relative of Henry Janney, of this city?" "I believe he is first cousin of my father." "Not long after I came here as I was walking down the Avenue [*i.e.*, Pennsylvania Avenue] the thought occurred to me that I needed a pair of boots, and seeing the name Henry Janney at the door of a shoe store, I thought there is a Quaker and an honest man and upon going in I met Henry Janney himself and had a very satisfactory talk with him. I found him so intelligent that I asked him to call on me, which he did and let me say to you that of all the men in this city whose acquaintance I have made there is not one in whose wisdom and intelligence I have more confidence than in Henry Janney." In writing his son, after the death of his father, I related this conversation and his mother expressed great gratification at it.

> In the late 1920's, Samuel M. Janney's granddaughters, who lived in Lincoln, formerly called Goose Creek, had a mass of old papers in a loft. Among them was one reading, as the editors recall, "Allow the bearer, Samuel M. Janney, to cross the Potomac at any time. A. Lincoln." The door of the loft was not locked, and the paper eventually "disappeared."

One of the most satisfactory memories of my life is that I knew Abraham Lincoln and knew him on such terms that he always saw me most cordially.

APPENDIX A

John Janney's Family

Jacob and Hannah Janney, the first generation in Loudoun County, Virginia, had twelve children, one of whom was a son named Blackstone. Blackstone and his wife, Mary Nichols Janney, had as their third son Thomas Jefferson Janney.

Thomas married Mary Taylor, daughter of Mahlon K. and Mary Stokes Taylor. Thomas and Mary had one child, John Jay Janney, the author of these memoirs. He was born on April 25, 1812, a month to the day before the death of his father. Thomas's widow was married a second time, on November 4, 1819, to Seth Smith. She left John, then aged seven and a half, with her parents—and, after her father died, with her brother, Mahlon K., Jr., who inherited the farm.

In 1835, several years after he had left for Ohio, John married his stepsister, Rebecca Ann Smith, the daughter of Seth Smith. The couple had five children and nine grandchildren.

Samuel Carroll Derby, Professor of Latin at Ohio State University, married the Janneys' daughter Frances in 1883, and John and Rebecca seem forthwith to have moved in with them. Rebecca died in 1886, and Frances in 1892, but John continued to live with his son-in-law in his Columbus, Ohio, home until early in 1902, when he was probably shifted to a nursing home of some kind. Whatever it was, he did not think highly of the food, from hints we get throughout his memoirs. When John's two grandchildren through the Derbys died young, he had outlived all his descendants except two far-away granddaughters.

John Janney was born near what is now Lincoln, Va., grew to manhood near what is now Purcellville, Va., lived most of his life in Ohio, and died in Columbus on December 11, 1907.

APPENDIX B

A Note for Those Interested in Texts

Some time in or just before 1900, John Jay Janney got a tidy red-leather record book and began setting down his memories of his early life. On rereading, he deleted about 10 pages of repetitions and expanded a number of items on the backs of slips cut from printed forms dated "Sept.   1888" that promoted the celebration of the Ohio Centennial held at Columbus. These slips he tipped into the book with glue. He had occasion to mention the date of writing several times in parentheses— (1900) and (1901). On page 189 he closed his work. This manuscript is owned by Mr. Edmund Derby Haigler, grandson of one of the step-granddaughters for whom John was writing.

This was apparently a rough draft. Though a neat worker, he scratched through, wrote above, and amended at will. Shortly thereafter, it would appear, he prepared from this draft another one, 119 pages long, in a journal now in the possession of the Bancroft Library of the University of California at Berkeley. The library received it from Mrs. Thomas Brown of Berkeley, daughter of John's son, Thomas Jefferson. This text copies the wording of the first draft—including the material inserted on slips—and the very dates in parentheses — "(1900)," for instance, at least once. It changes the original record and enlarges too, and contains its own share of tipped-in additions as well as sections on later life in Ohio and interviews with Abraham Lincoln. This might well be the copy that John says was "destroyed" after the drowning of his grandson Walter.

In 1907, the year of his death, John completed the third copy of his memoirs, 72 pages long, written on larger paper than either of the others. This book, like the original draft, is owned by Mr. Haigler. John's handwriting had become crabbed and shaky, and even without the date inserted here and there and the statement that it was completed in his 95th year, it is obviously the last of the three.

It is equally obvious, from a comparison of the texts, that neither the second nor the third draft copied the other but that they were each copied independently from the first. Each has its own emendations and enlargements that do not occur in the other, though in both of them John sometimes makes the same changes in substance.

After a text had been established from the two manuscripts in the possession of Mr. Haigler, the editors learned of the third text in the Bancroft Library. Since this proved to be copied from the earlier of the Haigler manuscripts, no major alterations needed to be made, but a number of doubtful readings could at last be resolved, and a number of illuminating passages became available, scattered throughout the work. Most valuable proved to be the afterthoughts John inserted on slips of paper into the Bancroft manuscript after he had written it, and the several pages of miscellaneous items toward the end that he set down as they occurred to him. Half the 18 insertions concerned topics not elsewhere touched on, and most of the others—like the miscellaneous pages—threw new light on matters already discussed. We thank Miss Estelle Rebec, Head of the Manuscripts Division of the Bancroft Library, for allowing us to use this trove of new material.

The Haigler texts, however, form the basis of the present work. The differences in substance between the two are slight in the main, though each has some fairly long passages that do not occur in the other. Where the texts cover the same material, the wordings are, for the most part, *nearly* the same—but only nearly. In detail, they tend to differ continually, and there are many places where one text gives significant information not found in the other.

One cannot, then, simply reprint one text as the "correct" one, nor can one simply shuffle together the "best" paragraphs, choosing first from one text and then from another. The differences are too integral a part of the sentences themselves for such a course. If all the texts were not to be printed in their entirety, which would make this a production merely for specialists, there was only one course left. The editor of the text, Werner Janney, has taken the unusual step, which he trusts the reader will condone, of amalgamating the texts into one, somewhat as daring scholars in the past have on occasion made a single text of the Four Gospels. My aim has always been to be faithful to John's own words, and so I have permitted myself few alterations of the original wording, except for the substitution of pronouns for nouns that would otherwise have to be repeated in an un-English fashion, and the dropping of words that repeated those of the other text. John loved long sentences tied together with *and*'s, and these *and*'s have been pruned ruthlessly. John was an old man, and he more than once simply skips an essential word. When obvious, it has been inserted without comment; when conjectural, it has been put in brackets. Brackets have also been used when words have been changed or added to keep the amalgamation grammatical, or when explanatory words have been inserted.

A brief example of what has been done may make matters clearer. The bleaching of muslin is discussed on page 140 of the earlier Haigler manuscript and again on page 153 of the same book. The two texts read as follows (note how, in the first version, John typically omits a word—the "a" of "a yard wide"):

p. 140

Bleached shirting could not be had for less than twenty five or thirty one and a quarter cents per yard, and unbleached or "brown" muslin yard wide cost not less than eighteen and three quarter cents per yard, or "three fips." It was spread on the grass, in the meadow, and with a "watering pot" (we had no "sprinklers") wet several times a day, while the sun shined, and was thus bleached quite white in a short time.

p. 153

Good bleached muslin could not be bought for less than twenty five or thirty one and a quarter cents a yard ("four fips" or "five fips"); and good sheeting, unbleached or "brown," cost "three fips," or eighteen and three quarter cents a yard. It was spread on the grass, usually in the meadow, and wet with a "watering pot," (we had not heard the word "sprinkler") while the sun was shining, at frequent intervals during the day. It could be thus bleached quite white in a few days.

In order to make one text of the two and yet retain all the information given in either, they were, admittedly more or less arbitrarily, amalgamated as:

'Good bleached muslin shirting could not be had for less than twenty five or thirty one and a quarter cents a yard ("four fips" or "five fips"), and good muslin sheeting, unbleached or "brown," a yard wide, cost "three fips," or eighteen and three quarter cents a yard. It was spread on the grass, usually in the meadow, and wet with a "watering pot" (we had not heard the word "sprinkler") while the sun was shining, at frequent intervals during the day. It was thus bleached quite white in a few days.'

Now and then the texts directly contradict one another. In such cases, the earliest text has generally been adopted as the standard, with a footnote alerting the reader.

As John makes plain, he was a perfectionist, and little things mattered to him. His organization is therefore good, taken as a whole. Nonetheless, he has a tendency to throw in items as he thinks of them, especially toward the end of his last text, written with sputtering pen and shaking hand at the age of 95. I have done what I am sure John would have eventually done: I have transferred straying items to the places where they belong.

John Janney's memories have survived because several generations, who have not even been related to him by blood, have cared about them. His daughter, Frances, married Samuel C. Derby, professor of Latin at Ohio State University, and became the stepmother of Derby's daughter, Florence Harlow Derby. As he has recorded, it was with the Derbys that John spent most of his last years. Florence became the mother of Edmund D. Haigler, of Hatboro, Pennsylvania, who has carefully preserved the two manuscripts and has been happy to let them be used here. Mrs. Edmund Haigler must be especially thanked for her loving care in transcribing the texts and discerning the meaning of many nearly illegible words. The manuscripts themselves were made available to me by the Haiglers, but she had already solved many of the riddles.

Werner Janney

BIBLIOGRAPHY

Janney, John Jay. *Autobiography of John J. Janney: How a family of Quakers lived in Virginia, nearly one hundred years ago.* Manuscript, dated in text 1900 and 1901. Written in a ledger, red leather, 8 x 5 in., pages numbered 1-231. Text occupies pp. 1-189. Each page ruled with 25 lines. Many interleavings and interlinings. Some sections repeated with slight variations, pp. 140-153, crossed through and marked "Dup."

Janney, John Jay. *A Sketch of My Earlier Bibliography.* Manuscript at the Bancroft Library of the University of California at Berkeley. 9 1/2 in., 164 pp.; A *Sketch* occupies pp. 1-119. Numerous insertions tipped in. Fundamentally the same text as the first except for the new insertions and an additional six pages on his life in Loudoun. Seen in microfilm.

Janney, John Jay. *Autobiography of John J. Janney: This copy written in his 95th year.* Manuscript written in a ledger, black cloth, le. corners, 9 7/8 x 7 3/8 in. Pages numbered 1-100. Text occupies pp. 1-78 with pp. 67-72 blank. "Interviews with Abraham Lincoln," pp. 73-78. 29 rules per page. Handwriting much deteriorated, crabbed and harder to read. Ink sputters.

Janney, John Jay. "My Grandmother's Garden." Proceedings of the Columbus Horticultural Society, Vol. 1, 1886, pp. 111-114.

Aikman, Lonnelle, *Nature's Healing Arts: From Folk Medicine to Modern Drugs.* Washington, D.C., 1977.

[Baltimore Yearly Meeting of Friends]. *Extracts from the Minutes of our Yearly Meeting, held in Baltimore, by Adjournments, From the Twenty-fifth of the Tenth Month to the Twenty eighth of the same, inclusive, 1824.*

Beach, S[tanley] A[mbrose], *et al. Apples of New York,* Albany, 1905, 2 vols.

Binns, John A., of Loudon County, Virginia, Farmer. *A Treatise on Practical Farming.* Frederick-town, Maryland, 1803.

Brewer, E. Cobham, Ll.D. Dictionary of Phrase and Fable. Giving the Derivation, Source, or Origin of Common Phrases, Allusions, and Words that have a Tale to Tell. Philadelphia, J.B. Lippincott & Co., n.d.

The Discipline of the Society of Friends of Western Yearly Meeting. Revised 1865. Indianapolis, 1866.

Rules of Discipline and Advices of Baltimore Yearly Meeting of Friends, Held on Lombard Street. Baltimore, 1881.

Rules of Discipline of Indiana Yearly Meeting of the Religious Society of Friends. Revised in 1892. Richmond, Ind., 1893.

Earle, Alice Morse. *Customs and Fashions in Old New England (1893)*
                              The Costume of Colonial Times (1894)
                              Colonial Days in Old New York (1896)
                              Home Life in Colonial Days (1898)
                              Child Life in Colonial Days (1899)
                              Two Centuries of Costume (1903)
Dates are those of original editions. All were in print, 1977.

Fielder, Mildred. *Plant Medicine and Folklore.* ((New York, 1975).

Hallowell, Benjamin. *Autobiography.* Philadelphia, 1883.

Harrison, Fairfax. *Landmarks of Old Prince William: A Study of Origins in Northern Virginia.* Richmond, 1924. 2 vols.

Head, James W. *History and Comprehensive Description of Loudoun County, Virginia.* N.p., 1908.

Heitman, Francis B. *Historical Register . . . of the U.S. Army.* Washington, D.C., 1903.

Hinshaw, William Wade. *Encyclopedia of American Quaker Genealogy.* Vol. VI, *Virginia.* Baltimore, 1973.

Janney, Asa Moore and Werner. *The Composition Book: Stories from the Old Days in Lincoln, Virginia.* Bethesda, Md., and Lincoln, Va., 1973.

Janney, Mahlon Hopkins. Unbound notebooks containing his files on Janney genealogy now at the National Genealogical Society, Washington, D.C.

Janney, Samuel M. *Memoirs of Samuel M. Janney, Late of Lincoln, Loudoun County, Va., A Minister in the Religious Society of Friends (Written by Himself.)* Philadelphia, 1881.

Johnson, Allan, and Dumas Malone, eds. *Dictionary of American Biography.* New York, (1964). 11 vols.

Johnson, Clifton. *Old-time Schools and School-books.* N.Y., 1935.

Krochmal, Arnold and Connie. *A Guide to the Medicinal Plants of the United States.* New York, (1973).   (1973.

Krochmal, Arnold; Walters, Russell S.; Doughty, Richard M. *A Guide to Medicinal Plants of Appalachia.* Agriculture Handbook No. 400. Washington, D.C., U.S. Gov't Printing Office, (1971).

Lamb, H.H. *Climate: Present, Past and Future.* Vol. 2: *Climatic History and the Future.* London, 1977.

Lewis, John G. and Elisabeth D. *The Minor Bartlow House, Loudoun County, Hamilton, Virginia: 1744-1970.* Hamilton, 1970.

Matthews, Samuel W. "What's Happening to Our Climate?" *National Geographic,* November, 1976, pp. 576-615.

McGraw-Hill Encyclopedia of Science and Technology, New York, 1971. Vol. 13: *Textile.*

Nietz, John A. *Old Textbooks.* Pittsburgh, 1961.

Ohio State Journal, Columbus, Ohio. Issue for April 5, 1907.

Poland, Charles P., Jr. *From Frontier to Suburbia.* Marceline, Mo., 1976.

Price, Steven D. *Take Me Home: The Rise of Country and Western Music.* New York and Washington, 1974.

Rau, Henrietta A. Diers. *Healing With Herbs, Nature's Way to Better Health.* New York, 1968.

Scheel, Eugene M. *The Story of Purcellville, Loudoun County, Virginia.* Purcellville, 1978.

Stoutenberg, Adrien. *A Vanishing Thunder: Extinct and Threatened American Birds.* Garden City, New York, 1967.

Taylor, Yardley. *Map of Loudoun County, Virginia, from Actual Surveys.* Philadelphia, 1853. Original: printed surface 36 x 50 in. Republished 1976 by A.M. and W.L. Janney, Lincoln, Va.: 26 x 35 in. Houses, churches, stores, mills, etc. are located, with owners' names when applicable.

Taylor, Yardley. *Memoir of Loudon County.* Leesburg, Va., 1853.

Whiffen, Marcus. *The Eighteenth Century Houses of Williamsburg.* Williamsburg Architectural Study Series. Williamsburg and New York, 1960.

Williams, Harrison. *Legends of Loudoun: An Account of the History and Houses of a Border County of Virginia's Northern Neck.* Richmond, 1938.

BIBLIOGRAPHICAL AND TEXTUAL NOTES

"BL" indicates the passage has been taken from the manuscript of John J. Janney's *A Sketch of My Earlier Biography* at the Bancroft Library of the University of California, Berkeley. Permission to use the excerpts is gratefully acknowledged.

1   BL: The entire Lafayette passage.

2   BL: Passage from "the back of a chair" through "the top one."

3   BL: "under which was the kitchen closet...fifteen inches in diameter."

4   BL: "above the fire place."

5   BL: "in every kitchen."

6   BL: "usually long ones—whence its name—."

7   BL: "A 'gridiron'...part of our diet."

8   BL: "To clear out...on the oven floor."

9   So the earlier text in the possession of Edmund D. Haigler. The later Haigler text of 1907 reads: "On special occasions we had custard pie, which I recollect with pleasure. It was not the custard you get at public tables today, but rich and lucious." Had the passage of a few years glorified the childhood dessert, had the writer attended too many public dinners, or was he contrasting the egg custard of his boyhood with the cornstarch pudding of a nursing home?

10   BL: "sometimes sweetened to taste."

11   Alice Morse Earle, *Home Life in Colonial Days*, New York, 1898, p. 143.

12   *Ibid*, p. 144.

13   BL: "Some used roasted rye....eight miles off."

14   In all three texts, John makes it clear that they stuffed the long, or "small," intestine. The earliest, however—and the Bancroft text, which copies it—states that this would be "about three feet long." Obviously a hasty error: That is the length of the large intestine. Also, though John does not say so, it is probable that the intestines were put into the brine *after* being turned inside out, else the brine would have soon become too filthy to be used.

15   BL: "for market or."
16   BL: The sentence.
17   BL: The sentence.
18   BL: The sentence.
19   BL: "We had no 'fly papers'...Both were effective."
20   BL: "which took about a week."
21   BL: "In the wagon trough. . . as they do now."
22   BL: The entire paragraph about traffic on the "big road."
23   BL: "We had three. . . pulverized alum."
24   Earle used the item in both *Home Life in Colonial Times,* p. 119, and *Old New York,* p. 131. The Gowanus oysters were being eaten, of course, in Brooklyn.
25   BL: "but we got only 'skim-milk.'"
26   BL: The paragraph.
27   BL: "was thirty years old."
28   BL: The sentence.
29   BL: "quails."
30   BL: The three paragraphs on quail.
31   The earlier Haigler text reads: "Eels were common in the large creeks."
32   BL: "Rabbits. . . snares."
33   The later Haigler text reads: "fifteen or twenty years before."
34   BL: The entire paragraph.
35   Quotations are from Alice Morse Earle's *Customs and Fashions in Old New England.* They may be found in the reprint by Charles E. Tuttle Co., Rutland, Vt. 1973, p. 34.
36   BL: The seven paragraphs on children's books and illustrations.
37   BL: The paragraph.
38   This is the only reference the editors have found in the literature to the log construction of the first Goose Creek Meeting House, built in 1750-51, though its remains were still to be seen when the editors' father was a boy.
39   BL: The paragraph.
40   BL: The paragraph.
41   John misread the entry in Rev. E. Cobham Brewer's famous old book. Brewer actually points out that the first part of the word "buckwheat" descends from older English *boc,* meaning "beech," related to German "Buche."

42   BL: "Farmers generally . . . witchcraft left."
43   BL: "their hogs were kept in."
44   BL: The paragraph.
45   BL: The two paragraphs on tar.
46   BL: The sentence.
47   BL: The paragraphs on the trundle bed and on the warming pan.
48   BL: "and one in two bed rooms, a dozen 'windsor' chairs."
49   BL: The paragraph.
50   BL: The paragraph.
51   BL: The paragraph.
52   BL: The last three verses of the song.
53   BL: "in gossip."
54   BL: "Carter, who . . . a son."
55   BL: The paragraphs beginning "We did not have the reverence" and "I did not know of any church."
56   As usual, Earle reground her grist in more than one book. The meat of this paragraph can be found in *Home Life in Colonial Days,* and especially on p. 369 of the Tuttle edition of *Customs and Fashions in Old New England.*
57   *Rules of Discipline and Advices of Baltimore Yearly Meeting of Friends, Held on Lombard Street.* Baltimore, 1881, p. 57.
58   *Ibid.,* pp. 58-9. The material that follows, including quotations, is drawn, with minor alterations, from pp. 55-69 on Marriages.
59   Earle, *Old New England,* p. 71.
60   *Ibid.,* p. 74.
61   BL: The sentence.
62   Earle, *Home Life in Colonial Days,* p. 198.
63   The earlier Haigler text and BL read: "The buttons for trousers were horn. . . ." The 1907 text reads: "The buttons for our women were many of them horn. . . ."
64   Words quoted have not been traced.
65   The two quotations are from Earle's *Costume of Colonial Times,* pp. 259 and 263 of the 1917 New York edition.
66   *Ibid.,* p. 242.
67   BL: The sentence.
68   *Costume,* pp. 237-8.
69   1907 text: "strong sail cloth."
70   *Costume,* p. 252.

71   Cited by Earle in *Two Centuries of Costume* as from *Rivington's New York Gazette.*

72   Earle, *Costume of Colonial Times,* p. 198.

73   1907 text: "on the top of the head."

74   BL: The two paragraphs from "At that time" through "and so on."

75   BL: "John."

76   From here the text follows the conclusion of the 1907 Haigler text, the version of his autobiography that John wrote when he was 95 years old.

77   The old man's handwriting is quite hard to decipher in places. Here he seems to write "surveys near under the Auditor's office" or "surveys near now the Auditor's office." Samuel Galloway, Ohio Secretary of State 1844-50, was *ex officio* the Superintendent of Schools and reorganized the Ohio system of public education.

78   What looks like "Secretary of State" has been altered to what may be "Auditor of State."

ABOUT THE EDITORS

ASA MOORE JANNEY and his brother, WERNER, grew up on a farm in Loudoun County, Virginia, near where their cousin, John Jay Janney, had lived as a boy. When they were young, in the 1920's, their life was astonishingly like John's exactly 100 years earlier. Werner left the farm to become an editor at *National Geographic*, where he also helped write the magazine's style book before he retired in 1978. Though he has retired as postmaster, Asa Moore continues to farm. He is also a bank president and a storekeeper. Both are Quakers; Werner is currently the Clerk of the Bethesda, Maryland, Monthly Meeting and Asa Moore is a former Clerk of the Goose Creek Monthly Meeting.

The Janney brothers love local history. In presenting their cousin's memoirs to the public, they share an ambition to "see that the work that John did actually accomplishes what he wanted it to do — let others know his way of life."